CAMPFIRE STORIES

THE SAN JUAN ISLANDS

CAMPFIRE STORIES

THE SAN JUAN ISLANDS

TALES & TRAVEL COMPANION

edited by
ILYSSA KYU & DAVE KYU

MOUNTAINEERS BOOKS

For our little barnacle and seal, Lula and Isla.
We'll always be your rock.

MOUNTAINEERS BOOKS is dedicated to the exploration, preservation, and enjoyment of outdoor and wilderness areas.

1001 SW Klickitat Way, Suite 201, Seattle, WA 98134
800-553-4453, www.mountaineersbooks.org

Printed in China

28 27 26 25 1 2 3 4 5

Design and layout: Melissa McFeeters

Library of Congress Cataloging-in-Publication data is on file for this title at https://lccn.loc.gov/2025932498

Mountaineers Books titles may be purchased for corporate, educational, or other promotional sales, and our authors are available for a wide range of events. For information on special discounts or booking an author, contact our customer service at 800-553-4453 or mbooks@mountaineersbooks.org.

Printed on FSC®-certified materials

MIX
Paper | Supporting responsible forestry
FSC® C188448
www.fsc.org

ISBN (paperback): 978-1-68051-756-9
ISBN (ebook): 978-1-68051-757-6

An independent nonprofit publisher since 1960

Contents

SAN JUAN ISLANDS STORIES

EXPLORE THE SAN JUAN ISLANDS

INTRODUCTION

A Garden Sanctuary in the Sea

WE ARRIVED in the San Juan Islands in early spring, just in time for everything to be caked in the pollen of bigleaf maples. Alder catkins loomed above us, their sneeze-inducing powder taking flight in the warm spring winds. To our delight, we enjoyed mostly sunny days and mild temperatures, not the gloomy, rainy weather we were prepared to experience in the Pacific Northwest offseason.

When life gets complicated, many of us dream of leaving modern life and its conveniences behind, perhaps starting a farm or moving to an island. In this archipelago of more than 170 islands scattered about the Salish Sea between the state of Washington and Canada's Vancouver Island, that life is possible. At least, in theory.

The San Juan Islands sit in the shadow of the Olympic Mountains, which block clouds and give the islands a more temperate climate than other gray and wet regions of the Pacific Northwest. This, in turn, allows for wildly varied landscapes, from coastal prairies and grasslands to oak woodlands and coniferous forests. Orchards, vineyards, vegetable farms, flower farms, lavender farms, and farms for livestock like goats, sheep, cows, and chickens all thrive here.

More than eighty of the islands are part of the San Juan Islands National Wildlife Refuge, established in 1976. To protect the nesting ground for seabirds, as well as the seals, wildflowers, and rare plants that survive here, most of these islands are not even accessible by boat, with a required 200-yard offshore buffer zone. Many of the other islands are inhabited by people but can be reached only by private boat or aircraft. Just the four largest islands—Lopez, Orcas, San Juan, and Shaw—can be reached by passenger airplane, seaplane, or ferry.

Though we had first mistaken it as just a form of transportation, we soon learned that riding the ferry to the San Juan Islands is an important *part* of the experience—a ritual, for many. From the comfort of the Washington State Ferry cabin, we enjoyed our view of rocky coastlines, catching sight of cormorants flying above and looking for orcas bobbing in the waves beside us. We learned this part of the experience is a sort of cleansing, preparing island visitors and residents alike for the slower pace of life ahead.

During our travels, we discovered that each island comes with its own personality. The largest, Orcas Island, attracts an adventurous outdoor crowd to its dramatic landscape and state parks. There are ample options here for kayaking, hiking, biking, swimming, and fishing. Breathtaking panoramic views of the Cascade and Olympic mountain ranges and neighboring islands can be enjoyed from Turtleback Mountain Reserve, Moran State Park, and the summit of Mount Constitution. Eastsound is Orcas's bustling town with restaurants, bars, bakeries, and shops. Those looking to be pampered off the beaten path head to Doe Bay Resort and Retreat or the upscale Rosario Village.

San Juan Island is home to Friday Harbor, the commercial center and county seat where many island residents do their errands—visit their doctor, go to the pharmacy, or stop by Kings Market for groceries downstairs and marine supplies and apparel upstairs, or to read touching tributes to dear departed community members on the storefront windows. Given the region's biodiverse marine ecosystems and its Southern Resident killer whale population, Friday Harbor is also home to the University of Washington's Friday Harbor Laboratories (a world-renowned field station for marine biology and oceanic research), the Center for Whale Research, and the Whale Museum, which is open to the public and also contributes to the research on killer whales. Outside of town in the rural farmland are farm-to-table restaurants, bakeries, historic resorts, and an array of parks.

Despite its relatively large size, San Juan Island is still a tight-knit community where neighbors look out for one another. While we were visiting a local farm, a car made its way down the farm's long drive, and its driver told the farmer, "One of your sheep is out! I noticed that your llama was looking really alert and then I saw the sheep running. The llama was like, *'Oh shit, the sheep is out!'*"

Lopez Island, which quickly became our personal favorite, is a creative and laid-back home to farmers, community activists, artists, and writers. The ethos of community and social justice comes through everywhere you visit here—through its many festivals, markets, performances, shows, rallies, and nonprofit organizations. It boasts jaw-dropping coastal vistas at destinations like Iceberg Point, Shark Reef Sanctuary, Watmough Bay, and Spencer Spit State Park; and its mostly flat topography and rural winding roads make it a popular destination for cyclists. Lopez Village occupies less than a square mile, and is best described in the piece "A Very Short Play About Lopez" fromNicholas Ferentinos's *The*

Islands: A Personal Portrait of the San Juan Islands. The entire play goes like this:

> "Pardon me, where's town?"
> "That's town."
> "*That's* town?"
> "That's town."

Last, we went to Shaw Island, which, at only 7.7 square miles, is the smallest and least populated of the ferry-serviced islands. Shaw's longest road runs roughly 12 miles, and "town" is the ferry landing, which consists of the Shaw General Store, the post office, and the only public restroom on the island, next to the car line for the ferry. Until recently, the general store was run by Franciscan Sisters, known and beloved by many as "the Nuns." Up the road, you'll pass Washington's oldest one-room schoolhouse, which in 2024 had a total of ten students from kindergarten through eighth grade. The island is primarily residential, but visitors can camp at Shaw County Park, visit Our Lady of the Rock Monastery, or hike the island's several preserves open to the public.

While we'd heard that Shaw's residents tend to be closed off and private, we experienced a strong sense of community and generosity. Here, people stop by the general store to get—and give—the latest news. The *San Juan Journal* quoted Terri Mason, owner of the Shaw General Store, saying that they have helped people find lost dogs and lost people, and with "flat tires, sinking or drifting boats, broken vehicles, keys locked in cars, flooded houses, bee stings, car accidents and even a bomb scare." One day, Mason related, she was working at the store when a man brought in a ball covered in kraft paper with wires and fuses sticking out of it. "I found this on the beach," he said, "and I didn't know what to do with it, so I brought it to you because I thought you would know." It turned out to be an unexploded Fourth of July firework.

• ✦ •

Outside of community, it's easy to get lost in the San Juan Islands' wildness—with so many ways to immerse ourselves in their landscapes and wildlife, we continually found comforting reminders that we humans are a part of, not separate from, the world around us. At the same time, some of our encounters with nonhuman residents felt so mystical and grand that we might as well have been on another planet. This was especially true seeing the region's most beloved mascot, the killer whale or orca—an apex predator that's not actually a whale but rather the largest species of the dolphin family.

It's no wonder the islands have become a renowned destination for whale watching. Witnessing whales in the wild is humbling and gives newfound appreciation for the accuracy of the only word we could muster after seeing them ourselves—*breathtaking.* Knowing and loving the San Juan Islands involves getting to know their orcas. Not just gimmicks designed to sell souvenirs to tourists, killer whales here are neighbors, friends, and family. Locals regard them almost like deities, and each pod and its individuals are as intimately known and beloved as family members. The Lummi people refer to them as *Qwel lhol mechen,* "our relations under the waves."

Resident killer whales and transient (also known as Bigg's) killer whales were once thought to be distinct groups of the species *Orcinus orca,* but scientists suggested in 2024 that these two groups ought to be classified as two separate *species*—confirmed not only by DNA but also by their distinct behaviors, family dynamics, diet, and communications. A trained eye can tell them apart by their physical appearance—resident orcas (proposed to be dubbed *Orcinus ater*) have rounded dorsal fins, while transient orcas (which could be labeled *Orcinus rectipinnus*) sport straighter and pointier ones. Resident orcas frequent the inland waters of the Salish Sea and are classified in two groups—the Southern Resident population (with their own distinct pods: the J, K, and L pods), often seen using the islands as a funnel to catch Chinook salmon returning to the Fraser River, and the Northern Resident population, whose territory stretches farther north in British Columbia and Alaska.

Sadly, orcas are listed as endangered in the US and Canada, and some even suggest they're headed toward extinction. One of the biggest threats to the San Juan Islands' Southern Residents is the overfishing of and destruction of habitat for salmon, their main food source. Killer whales and other marine mammals are also increasingly susceptible to pollution by toxic substances like PCBs (polychlorinated biphenyls) and PBDEs (polybrominated diphenyl ethers), and disturbances like boat strikes and noise pollution from the daily parade of ferries, cargo and container vessels, oil tankers, barge tows, and passenger boats using the Haro Strait, the Strait of Juan de Fuca, and the Rosario Strait as crucial shipping highways. In 2017, the Port of Vancouver began collaborating with the governments of Canada and the US, the marine transportation industry, environmental groups, and Indigenous communities to encourage all ships transiting the area to voluntarily slow down and stay distanced in critical orca habitat. In 2020, new rules for commercial whale watching were established by the Washington Department of Fish and Wildlife to protect the sea life, and other guidelines were issued by the Pacific Whale Watch Association.

One of our most memorable wildlife encounters in the San Juans was with another black-and-white mammal—but *on land.* After making a wrong turn while driving in the fading light of dusk, we screamed and hit the brakes as a dog-size black mammal with a white-tipped tail leapt out of the trees in front of our car. We had just enough cell service to confirm that we had witnessed a fox, and that the island's *red* foxes actually can be red, brown, or black. Common on San Juan Island, black foxes are rare in other parts of the world. These nonnative foxes were brought to rid the island of its problem with another nonnative species, the European rabbit, and the fox population has since exploded.

And then there are the birds of the islands. I, Ilyssa, have long resisted becoming a birder—perhaps in a desperate attempt to avoid becoming a stereotypical mid-thirty-something—but the San Juan Islands broke me. The many biodiverse habitats—which include rocky cliffs and sea stacks, forests, meadows, coastal prairies, wetlands, and ponds—along with the slow and quiet nature of these islands attract a huge range of birds and seabirds that don't seem to mind human presence. I was in total awe of the number and scale of the island's bald eagles, swooping on a hunt or perched above us, but what took me most by surprise was how much joy witnessing such wildly different seabirds in just a single beach stroll brought me. Some were picking through plastic debris along the shoreline, and other large groups seemed to be hosting floating mixers out on the ocean.

Not into birding? Just wait, the San Juan Islands will sneak up on you, too. One day something is just a duck or a bird, and the next you're debating if you've just seen a semipalmated plover or a killdeer, proudly jotting down sightings of red-breasted mergansers, least sandpipers, and rhinoceros auklets. The giddiness nearly knocked me off my feet each time I recognized a bird marked as "uncommon" in our identification guide, like a harlequin duck.

• ✦ •

With such incredible wildlife, great weather, and natural beauty, it's no surprise that the San Juan Islands are a popular destination. The islands' natural beauty and slow pace of life attract those looking for a simpler and quieter place to retire or raise a family, as well as visitors seeking a slice of island life. The islands thrive on tourism, but increased visitation is a double-edged sword. Precious island resources like water and solitude can be in short supply in summer, and a common sentiment we heard from service workers across the islands is that "either you have three vacation homes or you have three jobs."

While it's no surprise that anyone would *want* to live here, especially during the sunny and dry months of spring and summer, it's unfortunately not affordable for many, including young islanders whose families have lived here for generations, due to a competitive real estate market.

Walk around towns like Friday Harbor on San Juan Island or Eastsound on Orcas Island and you'll notice a line of shops and restaurants with "Now Hiring!" signs. The challenge, we learned, is not lack of interest in these jobs but lack of housing for workers due to the high cost of living and the limited housing inventory. A resident who moved to Lopez in 2007 shared with us a pet peeve that "everyone has gone to Airbnb," which is good for the tourist industry but not good for the workers who can't find anywhere to live.

Because of the tiny footprint of these islands and the number of private land holdings by billionaires like Oprah and Microsoft co-founder Bill Gates, there's only so much room for expansion while preserving the island way of life.

But the community is actively looking for solutions. The San Juan County Conservation Land Bank is a local government program that uses 1% of property closing costs to conserve and protect the special places that brought the community here in the first place. When we visited, the Land Bank had a network of thirty-nine preserves protecting over 5,000 acres for wildlife, recreation, and farming.

Rhea Miller, a co-founder of Lopez Community Land Trust, shared with us that for twenty-five years the nonprofit has acquired and held land in trust for the benefit of the community, typically as a means to permanently maintain affordable housing through home ownership or rentals. The model also supports agriculture, conservation efforts, and the development and maintenance of community facilities. She told us that the land trust model is flexible and "different for each island, depending on the needs of the community and the assets in the community."

Land trust models supporting agriculture can be a lifeline, as one local farmer explained. "It's increasingly difficult to make a living in agriculture, period, but especially on the islands where the cost of absolutely everything is so high. We have so many challenges with access to markets, access to animal harvest, and just inputs, supplies, all of that. Everything is just more complicated here." As farmers age out, they're finding fewer in the younger generations interested in carrying it forward, and that's where a land trust can step in. "As it's gotten [more] developed and farming has declined here, there's this real tension with everyone loving this pastoral beautiful landscape. They come here for the whales, but they also come here because there are these beautiful valleys and beautiful woodlands, and everyone wants a piece of that."

• ✦ •

For the people who call the San Juan Islands home, the glue that keeps them together is the central role of *community*. In every place we travel for the book series, we like to ask locals, "What do you hope comes through the stories in our collection that would give readers an authentic sense of this place?" People's answers usually describe the natural landscape and experiences in it. But here, every response was "the community."

If you dream of moving to an island to avoid other people, the San Juans are not for you. Locals love to joke about there being zero anonymity, and you couldn't commit a crime if you wanted to—there's nowhere to go. Shaw Island librarian Anne Frances Wysocki shared with us, "If you want to live here, you have to participate in the community. Some people come here because they want quiet and they don't want to have to deal with people. But we have an EMT service, we have a fire department, we have the library—there's a number of things that are *totally* volunteer driven. If you don't participate, how do those things happen?" Building a strong, engaged community requires a commitment to caring for each other despite differences. "Many people are very conscious of the fact that we have to live together here in spite of political differences, in spite of economic differences, or differences in personality. People think long and hard about 'How do we live with that? How do we keep relations between people?'"

It was the community and its traditions that charmed Anne and continued to lure her and her husband back for two weeks every Christmas—and the very same reason that brought them back to retire. Every holiday season, the school puts on a beloved musical for the island where something happens to the characters while *off* island and they have to get back on island. Through our conversation with Anne we learned of the many ways the community shows up for its residents: whether with meal trains for the sick or help with late-night plumbing emergencies; everyday gatherings like workshops, poetry reading groups, and weave and stitch nights; or annual traditions like the Fourth of July parade, the Christmas musical, and the school field trip fundraiser.

We learned it takes more care to live on an island. It always has.

• ✦ •

The Northern Straits region is part of the ancestral lands and waterways of Coast Salish peoples, which include the Lhaq'temish (Lummi), Mitchell Bay Band, S'Klallam, Samish, San Juan Tribe, Semiahmoo, Skagit, Songhees, Stillaguamish, Swallah, Swinomish, T'Sou-ke (Sooke), Tulalip, W̱SÁNEĆ (Saanich) tribes, and others. A subgroup of Coast Salish, the Straits Salish, inhabited and shared the bounty of the region around the Strait of Georgia and Vancouver Island, including the San Juan Islands. Yet their presence is hardly felt on the islands today. Amy Frost, executive director of the Lopez Island Historical Society and Museum, maintains that "it's really important for people to understand that there's actually a really deep Indigenous history here. As soon as the glaciers left about twelve thousand years ago, before there were cedars here . . . there were *people* here."

You'll find many memorials and place names that reflect Spanish, British, and American history and colonization, while Indigenous history and place names are remarkably absent. For example, Lopez Island is named for a Spanish pilot but is known to Coast Salish as *Sxwálech*, "the bottom of the reef net." Reef nets, *sxwo'le*, are funnel-shaped nets used to catch the midsummer-to-fall salmon runs as they make their way from the ocean to their spawning grounds in the Fraser River in British Columbia, a sustainable fishing method practiced for thousands of years by Indigenous tribes.

For many centuries, tribes in this region had overlapping territories and complex trade networks, practiced seasonal resource gathering, and shared a common language. But these rich fishing waters and farmlands inevitably attracted settlers, who came in part to strengthen the US claim to this region. They began to take over the land, waters, and resources on and around the islands—turning once bountiful, healthy prairies into grazing pastures for livestock, and the ocean into a full-fledged commercial fishing operation. With them, they brought diseases that devastated Indigenous populations, and nonnative plants and animals that impacted the biodiversity of the islands and the health of the soils, and prevented Indigenous people from gathering traditional dietary and cultural resources like camas. Some tribal members remained during the occupation of the islands, often intermarrying with settlers, but many others were forced to move to reservations.

Despite colonization, disease, and expulsion from their ancestral lands, Coast Salish tribes persevered. Their presence is evident at San Juan Island National Historical Park, which includes American Camp and English Camp, the defensive bases for the Pig War of 1859—a conflict between the US and Britain instigated by the shooting of, yes, a British-owned pig that escalated before being peacefully resolved through negotiations. Today, the park is working to highlight stories and histories beyond this somewhat glorified nonevent. In 2016, members of the Lummi and Saanich Nations dedicated a totem pole in honor of the hundred-year anniversary of the National Park Service. In 2022, a new visitor center in American Camp was created in close collaboration with the Coast Salish community to tell a more complete and diverse history, share the connection to the region's unique ecosystems, and show life before colonization. On display are traditional canoes and paddles, along with interactive exhibits teaching languages indigenous to the islands. The park also supports tribes in accessing cultural sites, harvesting traditional resources, and returning traditions.

The annual Gathering of the Eagles Canoe Encampment also launched in 2022, believed to be the first landing of Coast Salish canoes in San Juan Island's Shipyard Cove since the Treaty of Point Elliott in 1855. This agreement between the United States and two dozen Indigenous tribes ultimately forced Indigenous people—through duress and use of limited, unfamiliar, and codified language—to cede their rights to millions of acres of land, move to reservations, and abide by the laws of the US government even though they were not recognized as US citizens until 1924. The international border established in 1872 to settle the Britain-US dispute over the region split Coast Salish families between Americans and British rule. Amy Frost of the Lopez Island Historical Society and Museum told us that "tribes were no longer allowed to go to Vancouver Island to trade, and that's where half of their families were, so that border really divided communities." Meanwhile, increased commercial fishing led to more confrontations with settlers and fishermen. And government regulations, such as a 1934 law making it illegal to use fish traps, severely impacted access. While the treaty did guarantee tribes the ability to continue fishing, it was also used to restrict them.

Things didn't start to turn around for the Indigenous tribes here until the 1974 Boldt decision, a landmark court ruling in favor of the tribes that ensures they have rights to half of the annual catch of fish in their "usual and accustomed fishing grounds." While the decision was really good for the tribes, it also had a devastating impact on commercial fishing, which Amy Frost explains "was the lifeblood of the islands economically up until the 1970s. . . . It's a really sensitive story that we're still trying to figure out how to address ourselves." Nonetheless, the museum along with other partnerships and organizations are working to tell a balanced and complete history of the region.

Today, with help from community organizations and private donors, land is being returned to the Coast Salish people. In 2016, a private land owner donated 80 acres of Henry Island to the San Juan Preservation Trust and the San Juan County Land Bank on the condition it be used by the Lummi Nation for cultural purposes. In 2020, the same organizations acquired an additional 36 acres that will be protected from development in perpetuity by conservation easements on Orcas Island. The bulk of this land was added to the Turtleback Mountain Preserve, but 6 acres that are culturally significant to the Lummi people are owned and managed by the Lummi Nation as private property.

While honoring and reconnecting with their past, tribes are also leading efforts to address today's most pressing issues, like the impacts of climate change. The Samish Nation's Department of Natural Resources leads the research to understand the massive decline in kelp forests in the San Juan archipelago and partners with other agencies to restore their health. Kelp is a vital foundation of the underwater ecosystem because it provides shelter and sustenance to the microscopic plants and plankton that form the base of the regional food web. Contemporary farmers are drawing on traditional regenerative techniques used by the Coast Salish peoples for thousands of years.

What sets the San Juan Islands apart isn't just the peaceful lifestyle "away from it all." That masks a rugged resourcefulness necessary to make ends meet. Hardships draw people toward a shared understanding that the challenges of island living are better faced together. The collaboration, cooperation, and respect necessary to hold together the community mirrors the complex conversation of sea, strait, coast, and land. The San Juans draw their power from the beauty of a community working together to heal, preserve, and regenerate the land for future generations.

In creating this collection, we tried to gather a balanced mix of short stories, personal essays, and poems that capture this spirit across the San Juan Islands. These stories are meant to be read around a "fire," whether quietly to yourself from the comfort of your couch or aloud to the people sharing the ember glow of a campfire with you. While you may be expecting classic spooky campfire tales, these are not stories for those just seeking to be entertained, but instead for those who are curious about how certain special regions came to be and why they continue to mean so much to us—because the stories we tell shape our values and our future. The stories in this book will show you how to slow down to the pace of island life. You will learn about the wildlife along the islands' rocky coastlines, in their forests and coastal prairies, and in the straits and kelp forests that surround them; the history of those who saw the islands as a garden and those who came to build not just home but also community; and the complex ecosystems of land and water that make this region so special.

To identify themes and stories for this collection, we interviewed countless individuals who live and work here, and spent days inside libraries and bookstores across the islands. We hiked the beaches and coastal prairies, and visited museums, farms, and small businesses to fully immerse ourselves in the region's rich natural and cultural landmarks. We organized, researched, and wrote in the cabins of ferries traveling between islands. We sought recommendations and insights from locals and combined them with our own experiences to create a guide that offers practical tips on where to go, what to do, where to camp, and perhaps most important, how to visit in ways that respect and support the resident communities, human and wild.

Whether you've visited a hundred times or only through the pages of this book, we hope this collection deepens your connection to the San Juan Islands and highlights how fragile yet grand life can be and how it is meant to be savored. So, strap on those binoculars, hop aboard the ferry, and join us on island time.

Storytelling Tips

Storytelling has always been a fundamental part of being human. Beyond entertainment, stories have allowed us to share knowledge, traditions, and ideas, and to feel a sense of connection with people and places beyond our own experiences for thousands of years.

Through all its forms, we have witnessed how stories can create deeper emotional connections between people and the natural world. This is especially true across generations and communities who have been disconnected from the outdoors, yet who are, increasingly, responsible for protecting it.

We believe that stories are best when they're shared with others, so we encourage you to share any stories or sections you love with friends or family, continuing in the tradition of oral storytelling, by sharing them aloud.

Should you find yourself gathered with others around a campfire, here are some tips for sharing a story:

Be prepared. A campfire can provide a warm, flickering light that sets the perfect mood but may not be adequate for reading a book, so bring a lantern, flashlight, headlamp, or book light. A glass of water can rescue you from a fit of coughing or a dry mouth, so keep it handy. In a camp setting with crickets and a crackling fire, you may be competing to be heard—sit or stand up straight, breathe from your diaphragm, and project your voice.

Choose the right story. Choose a story that matches your audience's interests, age, attention span, and the moment. Pay attention to length; if it's too long, consider summarizing and read aloud only a particularly interesting or engaging poem or passage.

Introduce the story. Explain why you want to read this story, what it's about, and who wrote it—keeping it short and sweet. (Feel free to use our insider knowledge from the "About This Story" sections to get your audience excited.) End with a thought about what you took away from it and a question to engage your listeners.

Bring the story alive. Every story, especially poetry, has its own rhythm. When you read aloud, read it slightly faster than you would naturally speak but without rushing. Keep your listeners' attention by breaking up the rhythm with a long pause or a different cadence. (But don't overuse this trick or overperform!) Be authentic, enunciate clearly, and let your natural reactions enhance the story without disrupting the flow.

Most of all, have fun! Whether reading this book around a campfire, in your living room, at a park, or tucked cozily in bed, we hope you will find something that makes the natural world come alive.

Oh my island, my sanctuary, my retreat!
Let me find my rest within your boundaries:
Water-marked
Separate (and)
Alone

May I find peace on your shores
And release from the insanity of
Box-top houses
Instant food (and)
A clock-tuned life

Become my shrine, my holy place
Where I may worship
Freedom
Tranquility (and)
Serenity.

—NICHOLAS FERENTINOS,
"ISLAND PRAYER"

SAN JUAN ISLANDS

STORIES

Jewel of the Pacific Northwest

AUDREY DELELLA BENEDICT *and* JOSEPH K. GAYDOS

Excerpted from *The Salish Sea: Jewel of the Pacific Northwest*

The View from Raven's Roost

Ocean and clouds conjoin—a quintessential Salish Sea morning. Imagine, for a moment, your view from a clifftop aerie. The sea is the color of ancient jade. Rocky islets in the distance appear to float on luminous cushions of fog. The forest around you shimmers with raindrops, the air fragrant with the exhalations of Douglas fir and red cedar. A misty breeze riffles the water, carrying the evocative perfume of the sea at low tide. The raucous calls of black oystercatchers pierce the velvet quiet as they squabble over foraging rights to a newly emergent archipelago of tidepools. Suddenly, you hear a powerful whooshing sound and see a glistening black back and a tall dorsal fin—a male orca—cleave the smooth swell that lingers in the ropey fronds of kelp just off the point. Four more orcas surface in the male's wake, their smaller dorsal fins emerging in sequence as graceful as the opening of an oriental fan. Just as magically as they appeared, the five orcas blow in unison and then dive, disappearing into the depths. The clearing sky to the east reveals the snowy summit of Mount Baker rising above the fog like a ghost peak set adrift. There's no better place to be in the world at this moment.

Thousands of years before the first Europeans arrived in the Pacific Northwest, native peoples flourished along the shores of this magnificent inland sea. Named in honor of those first inhabitants and their modern descendants, the Salish Sea straddles the international border between Washington and British Columbia and includes the inland marine waters of the Strait of Juan de Fuca, Puget Sound, and the Strait of Georgia. Its waters embrace the southern end of Vancouver Island, the San Juan Islands, the Gulf Islands, and countless smaller islands. Oceanographers define it as an inland sea because it is largely landlocked, with the Strait of Juan de Fuca serving as the Salish Sea's primary portal to the Pacific Ocean. Tidal influence from the north, from Queen Charlotte Sound via Johnstone Strait and Discovery Passage, is minimal by comparison. The marine boundaries of the Salish Sea delineate all inland waters experiencing tidal exchange with the Pacific Ocean via the Strait of Juan de Fuca, creating an interconnected marine ecosystem that stretches from the south end of Washington's Puget Sound to British Columbia's Desolation Sound and the northernmost reaches of the Strait of Georgia. The Salish Sea is one of the world's largest inland seas, with a total marine area of about 7,000 square miles (18,130sq. km) and water depths in coastal fjords exceeding 2,000 feet (609m).

The Salish Sea is an ecological jewel—its remarkable biodiversity arising from the tide-swirled alchemy that occurs when land and sea are woven in an evolutionary fabric as old as time. . . .

Voyages of Discovery

Fog-shrouded days at sea remind us of the ancient mariners who traveled these waters without benefit of electronic charts, radar, or other modern navigational aids. Voyages of discovery have illuminated the spirit and captured the imagination of adventurers throughout history. The place-names we see on modern maps of the Salish Sea reflect hundreds of centuries of human interactions with both land and sea—a multilingual, cartographic narrative of Pacific maritime history. We tend to romanticize Europe's Age of Discovery, forgetting that the first European mariners to explore the Salish Sea were sailing into waters known to indigenous people for thousands of years. Coast Salish oral cartography names handed down from one generation to another—identifies places having geographic, spiritual, or tribal group significance. These names reflect the bounty of land and sea—the great gifts, or *S'abadeb*, in the Salish language. The lifeways and cultures that evolved along the shores of the Salish Sea are a celebration of ingenuity and brilliant adaptation to an ever-changing environment.

Salmon have always been the spirit food of the Coast Salish. The names given to major river watersheds, such as the Cowichan, Duwamish, Elwha, Nisqually, Nooksack, and Skokomish, delineate each tribal group's homeland and rightful claim to specific salmon spawning waters. In each case, the entire watershed was crucial to the annual life cycle of salmon as well as to the people who depended on the fish for their survival. In late summer and fall, thousands of spawning salmon filled these streams and rivers—shimmering streaks of silver, green, and red swimming upstream to their natal waters. At the end of the spawning season, with the scent of ghost salmon still lingering in the air, the coastal fishing camps were abandoned and people returned to the winter villages within the sheltering embrace of the forest—a watershed transhumance unlike any on Earth. . . . .

The Birth of a Sea

Reading the Rocks

The Pacific Northwest is one of the youngest and most geologically dynamic places on Earth. The volcanoes and mountain landscapes that frame the shores of today's Salish Sea were born in the regional epicenter of the Ring of Fire—the geologically active zone that rims the Pacific Ocean. The volcanic and seismic activity associated with this zone is the result of plate tectonics—a deep-earth process powered by immense geothermal convection currents. The planet's rigid surface is broken into 10 large oceanic and continental crustal plates and several microplates that are moving relative to each other and at different speeds over the underlying molten mantle. Without plate tectonics, there would be no ocean basins, islands, continents, mountains, volcanoes, and no Salish Sea.

Imagine the Earth's plates as a restless jigsaw puzzle of slip-sliding, diverging, and colliding crustal slabs. Where plates slip past each other horizontally along a fault or fracture system, frictional drag triggers stress-relieving earthquakes. Where plates diverge, ocean basins are created and basaltic magma rises from the mantle to fill the void along the divergent boundary and create new oceanic crust. When an oceanic and a continental plate collide, the heavier iron-rich oceanic crust plunges beneath the lighter silica-rich continental crust by a process called subduction.

The subduction zone serves as the crucible in which descending oceanic slabs undergo the ultimate geologic recycling—melting, dehydration, recrystallization, and eventual rebirth as new crust added to the overriding plate. Reading the evidence in the rocks, scientists are deciphering—episode by episode—the geologic and biological evolution of the Salish Sea.

The Salish Sea Story Begins

About 220 million years ago, the ancestral North American continent was part of supercontinent Pangaea, a single landmass surrounded by Earth's only ocean. With the breakup of Pangaea, tectonic events sent the North American Plate moving westward on a collision course with the Pacific Plate—a process that continues today. In the first act of the geologic evolution of the Pacific Northwest, the western shoreline of the ancestral North American continent was approximately where the Rocky Mountains are today. Over the next 200 million years, more than 400 miles (644km) of new land would be added to the northwestern edge of the North American Plate; today that land encompasses most of present-day Washington, British Columbia, and Alaska.

The spectacular geologic setting of the Salish Sea was created by two types of violent subduction at plate margins. When two plates carrying oceanic crust collide, the process of subduction builds an offshore arc-shaped chain of volcanic islands called an island arc. A continental arc forms when an oceanic plate plunges beneath the continental margin, which triggers volcanoes at the surface and the massive intrusion of silica-rich magma at greater depth. This collision-driven "docking" of island arcs and seafloor sediments along the continental margin was anything but gentle—more of a shipwreck of contorted upthrust rock. Geologists describe the setting of the Salish Sea as a complex mosaic of continental and island arcs. The extraordinary diversity of rock types on our beaches transports us back in time to distant mountain ranges and to the bottom of ancient seas. . . . .

• ✦ •

The mountain ranges that embrace the Salish Sea are dynamic systems in the still-unfolding story. The tectonic forces of volcanism, mountain building, and regional uplift that created Vancouver Island's Insular Mountains and the Coast, Cascade, and Olympic Ranges are forever keeping pace with surface weathering and erosion processes. As mountains in tectonically active regions erode, uplift occurs as hotter and deeper crustal rock moves toward the surface in areas where erosion rates are greatest. In the mountains surrounding the Salish Sea, higher elevation resulted in more precipitation, mountain glaciation, and ever-deeper incisement of rivers and streams—three of the most powerful erosion tools on Earth.

Water in all its forms—mist, rain, snow, ice, and glacial meltwater—serves gravity extremely well in sculpting landscapes. In fact, uplifts and their associated fault systems established the flow direction and drainage patterns of the modern river systems that nourish the Salish Sea. The Fraser River, regarded by some as the Salish Sea's most critical source of freshwater, reversed its direction entirely from a northward- to a southward-draining watershed system emptying into the Strait of Georgia—just one example of the many profound linkages between geology and biology that shape our world.

Fire in the Sky and Shaking Underfoot

Pacific Northwest volcanoes are a reminder of the Ring of Fire's youthful irascibility. Our stratovolcanoes—Washington's Glacier Peak, Mount Rainier and Mount Baker in the Cascades, and British Columbia's Mount Garibaldi and Mount Meager in the Coast Mountains—are sleeping dragons guarding the shores of the Salish Sea. Oral histories of the Coast Salish include countless accounts of fire in the sky and plumes of steam and ash along the saw toothed backbone of the Cascades and the Coast Mountains. Since the last Ice Age, for example, several dozen explosive eruptions have dramatically transformed the face of Mount Rainier. An eruption 5,600 years ago blew 1,000 feet (304.8m) off Rainer's summit to form a deep-seated magma chamber that continues to melt a labyrinth of steam caves beneath the summit ice cap. Mount Rainier's fire dragon sleeps fitfully, but ongoing seismic monitoring suggests that the volcano remains active and will erupt again.

Earthquakes are also a frequent reminder that the Juan de Fuca Plate is not finished with the Salish Sea. The Cascadia subduction zone, the major fault system located 47 miles (75km) offshore in the Pacific, defines the epicenter at greatest risk for a catastrophic earthquake that could affect the Salish Sea region. The 2001 Nisqually earthquake (magnitude 6.8), northeast of Olympia, caused significant infrastructure and property damage in Olympia and Seattle. A future megathrust earthquake could potentially devastate major population centers and profoundly impact the Salish Sea.

Finishing Touches: An Icy World

What we see today—the Salish Sea and its ice-sculpted backdrop—is largely the creation of the most recent Pleistocene glacial episode, the Fraser Glaciation. The saga began with the formation of a major ice sheet in the Canadian Cordillera between 30,000 and 25,000 years ago, concurrent with the last major advances of valley glaciers from the Coast Mountains, the Cascades, and the Olympics. The Cordilleran Ice Sheet spread south across today's international border 20,000 years ago, filling the ancestral Strait of Georgia and merging with glaciers flowing out of Vancouver Island's mountains and from the Coast Mountains, the Fraser Valley, and the Cascades. By 17,000 years ago, mainland valley glaciers had already begun to retreat in response to a warming climate. The Cordilleran Ice Sheet, powered by its sheer mass, continued advancing for several thousand more years, smothering the southeastern end of Vancouver Island, the Gulf Islands, and the San Juan archipelago in a stupendous blanket of ice. The Fraser Glaciation, which marked the final advance of the Cordilleran Ice Sheet, reached the north end of the Olympic Peninsula about 16,000 years ago, damming the Puget Basin with a wall of ice 60 miles (96.6km) wide.

The Puget Sound and Juan de Fuca Lobes of the Fraser Glaciation reached their maximum extent about 14,000 years ago, with the Puget Lobe pushing as far south as modern-day Tenino in the Puget Lowland, and the Juan de Fuca Lobe spreading west to meet the Pacific Ocean. During the glacial maximum, the Cordilleran Ice Sheet would have been nearly 8,000 feet (1.8km) thick above present-day Vancouver, at least 6,000 feet (2km) deep over Bellingham, and more than 3,000 feet (1 km) thick above Seattle.

By 13,500 years ago, the shift to a warmer climate caused the ice lobes to retreat rapidly, generating huge volumes of meltwater. The seafloor effects of all this water can be seen in the drainage channels now occupied by Lake Sammamish, Lake Washington, Puget Sound, and the Hood Canal. With the ice sheet in retreat mode, the Pacific Ocean flowed into the Strait of Juan de Fuca. By 10,000 years ago, the Strait of Georgia was also completely ice free. The three fjords—the Strait of Juan de Fuca, Puget Sound, and the Strait of Georgia—now formed an interconnected inland waterway dotted with islands both large and small. The Salish Sea was born anew, with a glacial imprint that would determine its future as one of the world's most biologically rich inland seas.

About This Story

We stumbled across a well-loved copy of *The Salish Sea: Jewel of the Pacific Northwest* in the used book sale section at the Orcas Island Public Library. Coauthors Audrey DeLella Benedict and Joseph K. Gaydos both have deep ties to this place. Gaydos lives on Orcas Island and is science director of the SeaDoc Society, a program at the UC Davis School of Veterinary Medicine dedicated to the health of marine wildlife and their ecosystems in the Salish Sea. Benedict, founder and director of the natural history education organization Cloud Ridge Naturalists, splits her time between the mountains of Colorado and an off-grid cottage on a tiny island in the San Juans. Their book, published by the SeaDoc Society, quickly helped us make sense of the formation of this region and how it has come to support thousands of different species of mammals, birds, reptiles, fish, and other sea creatures.

What we didn't realize about the San Juan Islands before reading this book is that rather than being an archipelago in the ocean, the islands are actually in an estuary—a partially enclosed area of water where freshwater rivers meet and mix with salt water—as they lie in the inland sea between Canada's Vancouver Island and northern Washington in the United States. The convergence of sea, straits, and rivers delivers an abundance of organic nutrients and sediment in the estuary's brackish waters, supporting a thriving marine ecosystem. The sea's unique geology, described in this piece, pushes tidal currents through narrow channels and past points of land, and forces water to swirl in what are called eddies; these eddies in turn bring nutrient-rich water and plankton closer to shore, making the San Juan Islands an especially good place to view marine life up close.

Following Skipjack

JILL MCCABE JOHNSON

From the trailhead at Obstruction Pass State Park on Orcas Island, my husband, our dog, Skipjack, and I head down the main trail a half mile to the campground and beach. Walking the woods here is a bit like time travel. Interpretive signs remind us that this land was once under glaciers. The Cordilleran Ice Sheet and its Puget Lobe covered the San Juan Islands and much of western Canada and the Pacific Northwest. The slow-moving ice scraped and exposed greywacke, a sedimentary bedrock formed four million years ago, and left in its wake a mantle of glacial till the ice had picked up in its travels.

Not unlike today's human population in the islands, the rocks we now see come from a diversity of places and circumstances. Archeologists and anthropologists are still learning about the various peoples who have lived here over time, and, in fact, less than half a mile away is the site of a recent discovery that upended our understanding of the history of the entire Salish Sea region. The finding came in 2003 when our friends hired workers to dredge their overgrown pond. With a backhoe, the workers exposed what looked like bones from a very large animal. Unsure what to do, and worried their equipment would cause damage, they carefully dug up the skull and dozens of smaller bone fragments with their hands. Under ideal conditions, trained archeologists would have handled the site differently, testing soils as they went and meticulously mapping the depth and distribution of the bones. To be fair to the workers, though, they had no way of knowing the age of the large animal they'd unearthed or its historical significance. What to the untrained eye might have seemed like a remarkably large American buffalo, possibly from a homesteader's farm, turned out to be *Bison antiquus*, a prehistoric and much bigger ancestor of today's bison. Using carbon dating, scientists later determined the animal had been killed and butchered by Paleoindians roughly fourteen thousand years ago. The reason this find was important to archeologists is because the animal provided the first evidence of pre-Clovis habitation in the Salish Sea basin.

I look at the forest around me and imagine how back then, when the glaciers had somewhat recently receded, we would have walked on grasslands and hunted for megafauna—all while staying on the lookout for the now extinct short-faced bear. Today, there are no bears of any kind on the island, except on the rare occasion when a juvenile black bear swims over from Vancouver Island in search of a mate. Each time it happens, wildlife officials trap and transport the young bears to the Cascade Mountains. On this late spring day, instead of a grass savannah, the terrain is covered by indigenous trees, shrubs, mosses, and other plants. Where the sun penetrates the overstory, it paints a shifting light show of sunspots. Western red cedars rise like entrance pillars to the park, evocative of the traditional poles the Coast Salish have carved in the coastal Northwest for thousands of years.

Our dog sniffs his way past mahonia and salal, while I crouch to inspect tiny wildflowers like starflower and sugar scoop. We have hiked every public trail on Orcas Island—including this one, a favorite—dozens, if not hundreds, of times. We enjoy marveling at the seasons, cycles, and ambience of these woods, how it shifts with the weather as well as from the plant life in varying stages of florescence and decline. A few weeks earlier, we would have seen chocolate and fawn lilies. Another few weeks will bring madrona tree flowers, strawberry blossoms, and Nootka rose.

Each section of the trail reveals different micro-ecosystems. Here, cedar roots crisscross the path. A game I have played since childhood is to make shapes out of the roots, like looking for shapes in clouds. Today, they appear to me like dozens of small, brownish-green crocodiles swarming through a muddy river. In childhood, my sister Jenelle and I might have challenged each other to dash down the trail without getting eaten alive. I can imagine us running across the backs of the make-believe crocodiles and pretending to stomp their long jaws shut to keep them from biting us.

Up ahead, woodpecker holes pepper a Douglas-fir snag. The elongated excavations suggest the work of pileated woodpeckers, who dig into the sapwood of dying firs and pines in search of beetles, carpenter ants, and other tasty wood-boring bugs. They often hollow out nests in the cavities of trees, too. This tree, whose top is long since gone, has rows of holes wending up the trunk from ground level. Well above my head are two larger, partially excavated holes, possibly the start of a nest that was later abandoned. We stop and, with the aid of an app on my phone that can record and identify bird calls, listen for sounds of a pileated woodpecker—its high-pitched, pulsing sound or its clucking calls that I swear sound like a louder, more fervent version of our brother-in-law's pet hens. The songbirds almost seem in concert with one another. Their trills layer and braid. I'm glad for the app because there are so many birds, I can't distinguish the individual calls—it identifies song sparrows, Pacific wrens, and orange-crowned warblers, but no woodpeckers.

Skipjack runs ahead as far as his retractable leash will allow. His yellow bandana flounces in jaunty contrast with his black-and-white-spotted fur. While he snuffles at the base of a red alder, I take time to enjoy succulents in bloom. The broadleaf sedum, whose Latin name is *Sedum spathulifolium*, loves this rocky habitat and has a yellow, starburst-like flower even brighter than the dog's bandana. The plants cling to the thin soil scattered among several larger stones lining this part of the trail. Nearby, *Castilleja hispida*, also known as harsh Indian paintbrush, blooms in a vivid orange-red atop long, hairy stems with lance-shaped leaves. I recognize this perennial that often stays green long after the other perennials fade in the fall, not because it has a longer growing cycle but because its roots are parasitic. I scan the neighboring plants to see which might be having their water and nutrients stolen, maybe snowberry or oceanspray, but without digging into the roots I won't be able to tell. Next, a patch of shortspur seablush forms a carpet of deep pink blossoms over leaves that look like wings on either side of the flowers' stems. At first, I mistake the ones in bud form for wild allium of the onion family, but once I see their petals leafed out, I know they are in the honeysuckle family. There are so many flowers in bloom on this day in mid-May, the bumblebees and other pollinators have plenty to savor, as do we.

Perhaps my favorite section of the trail is where a copse of big-leaf maples towers above. On sunny days like now, and especially in spring when the leaves are bright green, the canopy becomes a mosaic of brilliant greens that glimmer with light. I could stand dazzled here all afternoon, but Skipjack has spotted a Douglas squirrel partway up the trunk of a western hemlock. Resembling more of a chipmunk than the introduced red and gray squirrels, Douglas squirrels are indigenous and prolific where they thrive in undisturbed forests. This one barks sharp warnings to Skipjack, but, more curious than anything, the dog merely watches and doesn't bark back.

We continue on the trail through a small campground and to the beach, where we can now see a vast expanse of the earlier mentioned rocks left by glacial till, such as granite, quartzite, volcanic tuff, conglomerates, jasper, agate, and more. Many have been polished by their movement with the tides. Some expose jagged, broken edges. The overall effect appears to be millions of small pebbles in varying shades of gray, until we look closely and find tones of ivory, burgundy, and peach, plus creamy yellows and soft greens that range from sea foam to dark seaweed.

Today's especially low tide has revealed colonies of barnacles attached to anything sturdy enough to hold them. Although their lifespan is only about five to ten years, the crustaceans have existed on earth for at least 325 million years. The receding tide has also exposed tidepools rich in miniature sea life. Anemone tentacles riffle in the moving water. A frilled dogwinkle with its peach snail shell has bored into a largish barnacle to access the tender meat inside. Sea stars like to feed on barnacles, too. We used to see hundreds of a local sea star called the Pacific blood star in colors ranging from bright orange to purple at this beach. In 2013 to 2014, a wasting disease nearly wiped out the sea stars all along the western coast of North America. Fortunately, the population is on the rebound. With each visit to the park, we look for them lounging with their spiny rays lolling over each other, like how puppies flop in a heap after play.

The water appears calm, almost glassine. To the south and east lies Obstruction Island, beyond that Blakely Island, and in the distance across the Salish Sea, Mount Baker rises amidst the Cascade Mountains, still partially clad in winter's snow. On another day, we might see shorebirds such as great blue herons, kites, or the black oystercatcher with its bright orange beak crossing our view, but this afternoon we spot only seagulls who swoop and call with their plaintive, almost haunting cries. Two summers ago, we saw Southern Resident killer whales here hunting for salmon maybe a quarter mile offshore. The orcas glided along the surface of the water while whale-watching boats cut their engines and bobbed in the waves a respectful distance away.

Continuing along the beach, we admire various seaweeds such as porphyra, sea lettuce, bladderwrack, and bull kelp temporarily drying in the sun until the tide returns. When Skipjack begins foraging for dried-out crab shells, we know it's getting close to his dinnertime. We clamber up the stairs between the beach and campground, chat briefly with campers who've come from Bellingham across the water, then make our way back along the trail. We stop to admire fresh leaves on mahonia, or Oregon grape, and the bell-like flowers of salal that in fall form a hard berry the birds and other wildlife feed on come winter. I become fascinated by the wood grain inside a hollowed-out snag, like seeing a tree from the inside out. In the distance, the early evening sun shimmers off the water, and I'm reminded of the hour, how hungry the dog must be, and how hungry we suddenly are, too.

We'll return to this trail many times and will marvel once again at each plant and its cycles. This summer, stalks of foxglove will spring up in areas more open to sun. Digitalis, the heart medicine derived from these plants, has been in use for at least two hundred years and possibly as far back as the Roman Empire. I love watching how tall the foxglove plants grow over the summer as they shoot up more foliage and flowers. As summer progresses, so will the activity of dragonflies and damselflies whose names—blue dasher, spot-winged glider, vivid dancer—are nearly as charming as they are. By late summer, the sap of cedars and other evergreens will perfume the air. Come fall, my husband will notice fraying along tree trunks where rutting deer scrape the velvet from their antlers. I will look forward to when the bigleaf maples drop their leaves, which can be bigger than dinner plates. The multicolored leaves will coat the forest floor and soften our footfalls along the trail. And in winter, even if the trail is covered in the occasional snow, Skipjack will traipse happily onto the beach, sniffing out pygmy rock crabs, spiny red sea stars, and butter clams. We'll follow, hanging just as happily onto his leash, eager to make our own discoveries.

And who knows what other secrets this land holds? In the time since the nearby *Bison antiquus* discovery, others have been found on the island, and only a couple miles north of us, on Sucia Island, paleontologists discovered the first dinosaur fossil ever found in Washington State. While looking for marine fossils, they spotted a partial femur, or thigh bone, embedded in the soil with rock and fossilized clamshells. Eventually, the scientists were able to identify it as being in the theropod family of two-legged, meat-eating dinosaurs. Picture a smaller version of *Velociraptor* or *Tyrannosaurus rex* that lived roughly eighty million years ago, long before humans ever walked the earth. It puts our brief time on the planet, and especially our brief time on this trail, into perspective.

And yet, I can't help but feel a part of it all. Fleeting, yes, but I'm grateful to be here experiencing this moment in time, on this island, in a world layered with all that's come before, and ready for all that's yet to come. For now, I'm content with everyday marvels, like the time we watched bald eagles teach their adolescent young how to fish, or the day we encountered piebald deer with a rare genetic coloring that makes them more white than brown. I still hope to see the delicately mottled pattern of black, white, and yellow-green wings of the island marble butterfly, among the most endangered butterflies in the world, thriving once again throughout the islands as it flits along flower to flower.

About This Story

We learned about Jill McCabe Johnson after spotting her poetry collection *Diary of the One Swelling Sea* and an anthology she coedited called *For Love of Orcas* at Darvill's Bookstore on Orcas Island. Speaking to the folks at Darvill's, we learned she is co-owner of the Kangaroo House Bed and Breakfast down the road in Eastsound, one of the longest running B&B's in the San Juan Islands. Jill also offers this space for creative residencies, retreats, and workshops. We were thrilled to have her accept our invitation to take us along, with her words, on one of her favorite hikes with her husband and their trusty companion, Skipjack. She is a knowledgeable observer of the wild and wonderful things one might see along the way and also brings awareness of the millennia that came before.

Jill closes with a wish to see the island marble butterfly—a species found only in the San Juan Islands—thrive. Declared extinct in 1908, the species was rediscovered during a butterfly survey at American Camp in 1998 and was listed as a federally protected endangered species in 2020. Since 2008, Western Washington University and the US Fish and Wildlife Service have closely monitored this species, and the San Juan Island National Historical Park has maintained a captive breeding program to reintroduce adult butterflies into the prairie habitat. They can be identified by the green-and-white marbling on the undersides of their wings and are most commonly spotted on San Juan Island, feasting on wild mustard plants along the grassy coastline during flight season from April to June, though some have also been reported on Lopez Island.

Remembering Silé at Sxwelisen

RENA PRIEST

“We used to say, when the tide is out
the table is set.” With the glittering
turn of the tide, the arc of sun in the sky,
the call of birds, the sound of waves,
the spirit feeds us, the earth provides.

To be nourished in this way
makes that food on grocery store shelves—
behind doors that open and close themselves—
seem false, empty.

That food, where does it come from?
Whose hands grew it? Did anyone sing to it,
a song of thanks, of praise? Was there patience
and care? Were there prayers?

Think of how it got there—what it’s made of.
“When I was a girl, everything we ate
came from the earth that loved us,
through the hands of people we loved.”

Flourishing in the Seasonal Rounds

RENA PRIEST

To my ancestors, the islands of the Salish Sea were a garden. There is a tenet in anthropology that large, complex villages require agriculture. But on the coastlines of my homelands, since time immemorial, without traditional agriculture, we Lhaq'temish flourished. What does it mean to flourish? I think it means that the sun pulls you from the darkness of nonbeing, bestows on you the gift of life, and calls you forth to brandish all your beauty. If you have ever watched a time-lapse image of blossoming flowers, you will see that they sway and quiver, then explode like firecrackers, integrating and alchemizing sunshine—releasing it as their own shimmering radiance like light in the darkness.

To flourish means blooming, but it also means that although blossoms wither and fade, if they receive the proper nutrients they can come back stronger, more plentiful, and more beautiful with each new cycle. I believe the ancestors understood the cycle of flourishing and aligned with it to benefit themselves and all within that radiant circle. I believe this because for thousands of years, they enjoyed sophisticated foodways, a rich cosmology, and intricate artistic traditions without the toil of traditional agriculture.

In the winter months, they came together in large villages, while warmer months called for travel through the islands to all the beloved places, the usual and accustomed fishing, hunting, and harvesting grounds. Spring root sites, summer fishing villages, fall hunting camps. This way of life, our *she'lengen*, is known as a "seasonal round," meaning the people traveled in tandem with the harvests, moving with the seasons.

Cultural practices like controlled burns and selective harvesting ensured that the gifts of a particular place would return strong in the next cycle. The relationship to food was a direct exchange between the people and the Earth. There were no faraway factory farms, canneries, supply chains, ocean freighters, or exploited laborers. No grocery stores or cashiers to ask, "Plastic or paper?" Instead, the people had harvest songs, and as they worked they sang, while birds sang back from the trees.

The ancestors ate food from the island prairies, forests, and shorelines and accepted the gifts of a fond and loving landscape that poured forth a profusion of nourishment and beauty, and a feeling of well-being and connection. In our traditional diet, omega 3 fatty acids in salmon provide vitamin D—the sunshine nutrient that insulates people from the gloom of winter. Rose hips and berries give antioxidants, potassium, magnesium, vitamins C and K, fiber, and prebiotics along with their sweetness. Shellfish give B12 for vitality and energy. Wild game furnishes protein. Foraged greens and roots give minerals and medicines, and the seasons offer variety, the spice of life.

Every stop in the seasonal round offered new ingredients for the endless feast. Flowers glowed in the landscape like wrapping paper on a gift. When a camas flower blooms, it's your birthday. Dig in. Enjoy! Blossoms signal forthcoming berries—all kinds of berries: wild strawberries, black caps, trailing blackberries, salmonberries, thimbleberries, salal, gooseberries, huckleberries, blueberries. In lowland bogs were tart cranberries, and in the trees, bitter red elderberries; each berry type with its own dynamic benefits, from boosting immunity to suppressing appetite.

To hunters, the forests yielded deer, bear, and elk, while the sky gave ducks and geese. To gatherers, the landscape offered fiddleheads and the roots of licorice ferns, which chased away a sore throat. Cattail, skunk cabbage, and wild water lilies (in addition to camas) produced starchy roots that could be dried and saved as staples. Miner's lettuce and clover were eaten as fresh greens, while sea asparagus, wild carrot, and onion added complex flavors.

Streams provided clean, clear drinking water, and when the weather was cold, rivers ran with eulachon, whose oil was a welcome warmth, adding umami to the menu. Twice a day, the beaches gave such bounty that the people had a saying, "When the tide is out, the table is set." There were succulent horse clams, butter clams, little necks, cockles, and oysters. Nestled in the seaweed and shallows were tasty Dungeness crabs, octopi, sea urchins, and many other delectables.

In the cold, teeming waters off the village's doorstep, all you had to do was drop a hook, and up would come a ling cod or colossal halibut. Herring ran so thick that the people raked them from the water like autumn leaves. Herring roe was a delicacy to be savored. There were also flounders, dogfish, snappers, and perch. And, of course, there was the keystone species whose generosity sustained all life in the Salish Sea bioregion: the reliable and bountiful seasonal sacred salmon.

People of the sea sing in gratitude
with stories of how salmon give themselves

to nourish the people with sacred food.
For as long as salmon swim, all will be well.

Grandmother tells how out in the cold straits,
our most ancient kin, the Qwel lhol mechen,
sing "this is where the salmon run today."
Follow the beacon of the tallest fin
and you shall share in the bountiful feast.
This is how it was when we were still joined
in a web connecting greatest to least
with abundance for all to enjoy.
We sing to remember our gratitude
to the life that becomes our sacred food.

Around four thousand years ago, the ancestors devised an innovative technology called a reef net, the operation of which strengthened community bonds. The nets were woven by matriarchs who each contributed a panel to be sewn together like a quilt, ensuring each contributor a portion of the catch. The net was strung between two canoes anchored side by side. It had a hole at the top to allow for escapement. When the captain gave the word, the men in the canoes hauled up the net, and the catch was taken from the middle of the run, allowing salmon at the back to continue with fish at the front. This selective harvest kept the runs strong. The reef net design was modeled after a womb. When salmon swim up the false reef and into the net, they become the spark of life to carry us into a new cycle.

This cycle flourished for thousands of years and might have continued for thousands more, but in 1855, the Treaty of Point Elliott was signed. Despite the treaty's guarantee of access to our usual and accustomed fishing, hunting, and harvesting grounds, we were denied our rights and isolated from the garden—the gifts of our homelands, our beautiful way of life. We still maintain our way of life, as much as we can within the changes brought about through colonization, but of course, the garden is not what it once was.

How did our garden come to be? As an Indigenous writer, I am sometimes asked if I will write about our tribal prehistory. People like to hear our ancient stories. Of course they do. But those stories are not meant to be written. They contain wisdom accumulated over millennia. Their roots are sunk deep in the land and waterways. Those stories acknowledge the living spirit in every plant and animal that lives here. They are like etymology, explaining that *flourish* comes from ancient times and means "to adorn with flowers," while animals are called such because they are infused with *anima*—from the Latin for "spirit" or "breath," perhaps connected to the Greek *anemos*, "wind." To be animat-ed-animal-alive is to have breath, spirit. The beautiful flower we call anemone shares its name with the sea anemone, which translates from the Greek as "windflower" or "daughter of the wind." This name acknowledges a relationship between the wind of the world above and the wind of the world under the waves.

My ancestors also observed the blossoming of flowers and the shift of the wind. They acknowledged a relationship between our world and an unseen world under the glittering surface of the Salish Sea, home of the *Qwel lhol mechen*, "our relatives under the waves," also known as Southern Resident killer whales. Because of the unique culture of the *Qwel lhol mechen* and our ancient relationship with them in our shared homelands and waterways, we understand that their world mirrors ours; we understand that what happens to them happens to us. It's easy to recognize this relationship when you look at the similarities between their culture and traditional Lhaq'temish culture. Like us, *Qwel lhol mechen* are good at catching salmon. They follow the lead of their matriarchs and always travel together as a family. They are also known to sing and gather in celebration with neighboring pods. For all these reasons, their name acknowledges our connection, "our relatives under the waves."

We understand our world a little better by understanding how it is named—how it came to be known. And when we understand something, we are better able to love it. This is what the ancient stories do. They give meaning and anchor us in the world. A long time ago, some say as long ago as twelve thousand years, the glaciers receded, leaving a rocky, barren landscape. The majestic forests had yet to take root, but there was water—clear, cold water—and then salmon came, bringing all the rich minerals of the sea in their shining bodies. Everything partook of these riches and began to flourish. The ancestors came down from the Fraser River canyon and made a life in these islands.

Because it's good to understand something about this place and our relationship to it, that you might love and respect it as we do, I will share a Lhaq'temish story that I made into a poem with permission from my *oksale*, my teacher. The story is an abbreviated telling of a longer saga. It is not my story. I do not own it, and as a Lhaq'temish birthright it is not to be shared without permission from our culture bearers. My version is only an iteration in an ongoing, fluid, and ever-changing tradition. Like others in our oral tradition, this story has flourished—been animated by the breath and voices of many tellers over hundreds of generations across the region.

This is the story of Kwome and Kwelshan,
two mountains in my homelands,
and how through their parting of ways
the islands of the Salish Sea came into being.

A long time ago, the mountains were married.
For some reason, who knows why?—
one day Kwome decided it was time
to be on her way.
As she traveled, she wept,
and her salty tears
became the swirling eddies of the Salish Sea.
Soon, she grew tired and stopped to rest.

She set down her texwitch, her bow,
to have a bit of xwelol, camas,
and when she got up to go,
in her sorrow she forgot her texwitch
and dropped a little piece of her xwelol.
These became the islands the people know
as Texwitch, the island shaped like a bow,
and Pen'nex'weng, the island where we go
to p'aneq, to dig for xwelol.

She went along this way, leaving gifts
for the people. And the gifts have stories
to map the bounty of the Salish Sea.

When she arrived where she stands today,
she decided that was far enough away.

Sometimes on a clear day, you can see her
all the way from her old homelands
where once she stood with handsome Kwelshan.

He likes to catch a glimpse of her
glowing majestically in the rare sunshine.
He could look at her and nothing else
for the rest of his life. But soon she decides
it can't go on this way, and she draws the clouds
around her face to disappear back into the gray,

and that is how the ancestors explain
these blankets of clouds, the falling rain.

In my work, I had an opportunity to speak at an event in Canada. I shared the story of Kwome and Kwelshan. Afterward, a tribal elder (I don't remember which nation) thanked me for sharing. He told me Kwelshan was their mountain, too. He relayed a few anecdotes from their stories, and it made me smile to hear the affection with which the elder spoke of our shared mountain.

At a similar event on the W̱SÁNEĆ reserve in Canada, I noticed that some of their language corresponded to words I know in the Lummi language. The similarities were explained by a tribal elder with the aid of a large map of the Salish Sea. On the map, he circled a traditional Lummi village site out in the islands. Then he circled a W̱SÁNEĆ village site and drew a line between the two. "Look how close we were," he said. "You could get in a canoe in the morning and ride the current to be in Lummi land by the afternoon."

It was a lovely reminder that we are all connected in ways we may not even be aware of. We each are a part of something bigger. We Lhaq'temish have been here sharing this landscape, these waterways with the flora and fauna of the place for a very long time. We will continue to be here for a very long time. As the elders say, our human lives are just the blink of an eye in the creator's timeline. International borders, destruction of habitat, endangerment of species, and other consequences of colonization cannot last forever. Until then, may we seed knowledge of our rich heritage and make our minds fertile ground where a dream of natural abundance can take root in our collective imagination so that together, we might enter a new cycle of flourishing.

Notes:

Silé is "Grandmother."

Sxwelisen is a place name for a land bridge that emerges at low tide where we go to harvest shellfish.

Texwitch is also known as Eliza Island, and *Pen'nex'weng* as Vendovi Island.

About This Story

It's now a running joke that we're going to keep selecting locations based on their relationship to Rena Priest, whose writing we included in the Olympic National Park chapter of *Campfire Stories: Volume II*. Rena served as Washington's sixth poet laureate and is a writer, poet, editor, and member of the Lhaq'temish (Lummi) Nation. Struck by the lack of Indigenous presence on the islands during our visit, we were glad to get Rena on board to write about the Lummi Nation's connection to the islands and all of its living things.

We originally discussed a piece that captured the San Juan Islands as a garden, but after we reached out for advice on the Indigenous perspective on killer whales, or *Qwel lhol mechen*, Rena artfully wove in more about the gardens below the waves, too. She explains, "Because of Lummis' unique historical positioning in the San Juan Islands and outlying areas, along with the unique social and cultural habits of the Southern Residents, our relationship with them is very special." Rena's piece mentions the 1855 Treaty of Point Elliott, which altered the Lummi Nation's access to the land's bounty and had a permanent impact on these once-flourishing islands and gardens, above and under the waves.

Island Light

ANNA ODESSA LINZER

This Morning

As if poured from a clear glass pitcher, a stream of fog flows through the white blossom petals of an ancient apple orchard, falling over spring's green moss, peppered now with the blue of wild camas, until it cascades down the island's grey stone to cold pebbled shore. And low out over the still, mirrored waters, it becomes a smoky rushing river, catching the sunlight rising over Turtleback Mountain, to fill the bay and the morning with memory and desire, grief and loss. In the sharp curve of the narrow twisting road little girls and I ride the old dusty blue Volvo into the fog's muted shadow and light, then through and out to catch the ferry. Down the hill, we hear the heft and motion of the vessel's steel hull already straining thick hemp line as it creaks against wooden pilings, until the metal bridge clangs to the dock, echoing through the single sad cry of a foghorn. On the deck of the ferry, I catch the first glimpses of shimmery fog dancing in soft hair and on smooth cheeks of twirling girls, like stardust or moonlight or phosphorescence, knowing even then that it will enter their dreams and trail like silk streamers through their days. And I reach up to feel the strands of my own hair for the tattered golden remains of memory's gifts.

First Car on the Ferry

The heat of sun, and its long hold on land and water, spins us through this drought of spring-unto-summer, until it is as if the white of light and the blue of sky and bay will always and only be divided by green brushstrokes of fir and madrona, the dusty smudges of yellowed grasses, and bleached lines of drift. But with the clang of steel chains and thrust of submerged propellers on this floating metal seed pod, the Elwha casts us out into evening and the assault of water against glass.

> *Thrust: when a system expels or accelerates mass in one direction, the accelerated mass will cause a force of equal magnitude but opposite direction on that system.*
>
> As the hold of the dock is broken and we are carried into the bay by the blasting music of water and metal, through the windshield I see the fluid dance-on-glass as six cormorants hurl themselves as if wingless bullets, one after the other, just beyond the bow, perfect black silhouettes.
>
> *Silhouette: the dark shape and outline of someone or something visible against a lighter background, especially in dim light.*
>
> As if carrying threads of silk, they stitch across sky the line of a summer we now break to enter grey fog grey cloud grey rain and the floating world of black-against-grey islands. All else is lost.

In Each Seed

Ocean spray holds
summer's golden promise
made and soon broken
as the fickle sun begins to turn her face away
from the greens of this northern coast
taking heat and light
from hills and rocks splashed in jeweled colors
we lean into as if
these littered leavings
were warmth itself
until one day they too
will fade and fall into frosted light of winter
touching the black and white and grey of chickadee feathers
seeming to hang weightlessly
in the brown clusters of tiny seeds
once born by delicate floral perfume
that left behind the last prick of summer
light clutched tight
in each seed.

Shaw Island Local News

The deep sleep of a moonless night broken by the echoing, as through a long metal pipe or culvert or underground tunnel, or through the speakers of a movie house showing some sci-fi movie I'd never watch. I listen into wakefulness. And know then what night visitor is just outside our window. A fox. A warning cry I cannot decipher, but recognize it and all its fear as it scribbles its way through my veins with cold dark ink. The next morning outside the tiny post office I ask the small cluster of locals about fox on the island, knowing fox have not been here before, but also knowing that the stretch of cold waters and swift currents between us and the other islands is not too big of a divide for those of us who find our place in the world by swimming. My words are swiftly brushed aside. *Raccoon.* I say, *no it was the alarm cry of a fox*, and I continue about the fox scat I saw in the grasses under a summer evening sky in the ancient apple orchard on the preserve on the south side of the island. A man who lives near the preserve catches my eye, and speaks quietly. *Yes, a friend said she saw a fox there early one morning.* No one else speaks. I say goodbye as I leave, but first a nod to him. *Let me know what you see.* No other eyes meet mine. As a person of place—a place where I am no longer living, a *homeless person of place*, I joke—I understand that I have crossed a line. My violation has been deep. There are no words to be spoken about what I know. Only the cry of the fox that has lodged itself deep in my flesh and seared my soul in recognition. Swimming *from*, and then *to*, to save our lives, pulling ourselves, wet and cold and grateful, onto waiting shores that hold a beauty that is both unfamiliar and familiar but always beyond words, to find our way, to awake at night with a fear we can only scream, knowing that memory is the ghost that haunts us, that only we can see.

Light Seeking

The darkness of the path through
the forest at dawn
is broken only by the horizon's thin line of light
coming through the trees as if
splinters of light-throwing glass
are pulling the sun up and over the water.
Along the dark path I follow starlight
of ghost berries holding the light like fireflies

as they float free from their thin leafless stems.
I have walked this trail before,
but never once have I seen the ghost berry
dance, seeming to sing the morning in.
All the rest of my walk through
the forest I ponder, wonder at what I had missed.
The sun does not wait for me, climbing as it does
into full morning sky.
I cross the wooden bridge,
and I turn to return to the beginning.
But now the darkness is fully broken
and the trail is flooded once again in the wintered yellow
of salmonberry leaves.
The ghost berry stars have faded
back into wherever they go in the daylight.
At the little building, still darkened
for morning meditation,
I hang my jacket and sit to join
the others in the circle
around a candle whose light
and promise has already
slipped away into morning with the phantom
ghost berry.

Knitting Colors

In the circle of an island forest clearing edged with the Queen Anne's lace and Nootka rose, tall grasses and slender beach vetch dance around and above me to the soft whisper music of summer rising off the waters, as if on cue. A cobalt blue dragon fly threads through the tapestry of green stems, hulls of ripening grains, fading greens washed in mauve and amber, and delicate fabric of violet flowers, entering the weft and warp of design. I flick another piece of peeling black paint from the wide greyed arms of the low Adirondack chair that has already woven through so many seasons, so many homes of our hearts, and touch the smooth dark cherry-wood needles on my lap of twisted yarn. The sunlight of the last afternoon-into-evening of June weaves deep into the grasses. A coin-sized tree frog lands on my bare foot, a splash of lime green. I feel us both blink as if just waking from long winter-spring grey by this now-summer day. The small wool garments grow like the lengthening light, like the girls who will dance them through the seasons. A basket of jewel-colors, knotting one season into the next. And the next.

Thistles

Thistles along the edge of summer in burned grasses ringing the house, scattered among nettles and tansy, just above the rocks, before it falls away to ocean spray and wild raspberry tumbling toward the grassy meadow and the spring fed pond with its cattails and treefrogs and yellow irises to fill its days. And as I watch, as if on station, the thistles shoot up, send their fingers to the sky, elbows sharp and jabbing, I catch the flash of other sentinels. Goldfinches land in fir branches. Flutter down like leaves, land like butterflies on the first show of purple blossom, until so suddenly carried away on an unseen breeze, as if of their own making. And now the ring of thistles catches the ring of twirling yellows. A poem of such precision: ripening seeds held to downy wings, caught by the yellow finch. Just in time. Just on time. I glance at the pruners still in their sheath on the picnic table, then turn away.

Calendar

August burns deep into the heart of June. Grasses dry golden. Gone already to breeze: dancing seed. The pinks and yellows of madrona leaves are scattered on grass, on dirt road, along rocky shore. Freed from the dried rattling burdens of memory, the madrona turns away, the brilliant waxy gaze of new leaf holds only the sun. Patiently, silently holding branch and bright leaf, peeling red stems expose a green so tender and vulnerable, my heart aches. Air on skin, an August kiss. And so suddenly, so many Augusts come full to me, bathing me in their light of memory and desire, until I am homesick for days that I thought were long tucked away down the end of a washed-out dirt road, under cedar and fir and lichen and thickly silent moss. But here they are, with the wild goodness of salt spray and campfire smoke and green canvas sleeping bags, the first star in the night sky, Venus falling into morning's west. And like all August days—even these who have not yet arrived, but are already opening their packs, looking for the chocolate bars, the graham crackers—they will not stay.

About This Story

Anna Odessa Linzer is a writer and environmentalist who has spent a lifetime along the Salish Sea, working on protection and restoration issues, and founding one of the first land trusts in Washington State. In the 1970s she lived on San Juan Island, where she built a small home on the west side at the base of Mount Dallas, and later she divided her time between Shaw Island and Dabob Bay. We came across Anna's gorgeous *Home Waters* novel trilogy in the local writers nook of the Shaw Island Library and Historical Society, a tiny well-stocked literary collection on the smallest ferry-serviced island.

We reached out to Anna to see if she'd like to create something for the book. After careful consideration, she pulled together this collection of Shaw Island poems and prose, both unpublished and published in her 2024 book of poetry *Season Unleashed*, writings she describes as "fully present on the island." She goes on to say, "These pieces were written over the many years we lived there and they speak to the essence of the island I experienced. I find myself easily slipping back to Shaw as I read them." What underlies these vignettes that give us a rich feel for the natural world on Shaw Island is Anna's love of the place.

My Hermitage

GARY THOMPSON

I live on an island
in the Salish Sea
because I love boats—
that's what I say

when asked why I chugged
off the edge of the map
aboard *Keats*, and how,
deep in life, I stepped

ashore for R & R
and found my lost self
home. Islands are
like shells in the surf

of continental drift—
tumbled, some weathered
for eons, others
still smooth shelters

a hermit might crawl
into to be safe,
a portal he bears everywhere
like a dear gift.

The Mountain Is Out

GARY THOMPSON

On our usual walk today,
two juvenile bald eagles, floating
on the breeze, circled in and out of view—
first just above the cedars and firs,
then the meadow at the bottom
of the hill, and finally out
at Middle Point, where the Cascades gleamed
as backdrop and The Mountain,
as we say here, was most certainly out.

The morning throbbed with wonder,
or so it seemed, but of course the eagles
were simply hungry and hunting.
What would Professor Olmstead make
of that oft-dreaded pathetic fallacy,
my love? Still, when we reached the clearing
where the truck was parked,
there were six or seven of them wheeling
high up, almost out of sight,

in the surely awed sky.

About This Story

We came across Gary Thompson's book of poetry *Broken by Water: Salish Sea Years* in the local writers section at Griffin Bay Bookstore and Cafe in Friday Harbor on San Juan Island. These poems from the book give a glimpse into Thompson's life on the island and read as a love letter to place. (Professor Olmstead was one of his literature professors, who discouraged students from ascribing human emotions to anything not human.) Thompson and his wife moved to the San Juan Islands with their beloved trawler *Keats* in tow to explore their new home waters. Thompson told the *San Juan Journal* in 2021 that his hope for his poetry collection is that readers "slow down enough to hear the rhythm and sounds of the language, along with the history engrained in it."

It's common for locals to acknowledge when "the mountain is out," as the magnificent Mount Rainier is often shrouded in clouds or fog. Pictures of the snow-capped mountain don't do it justice. Its presence looming in the distance often provoked us to think, People just live here *all the time*?! As if the mountain weren't enough, the abundant eagles wowed us—soaring above us on the ferry, sitting regally atop Cattle Point Lighthouse, and even swooping along over our heads in a convocation of six or more as we made our way down a winding road on Orcas Island. As captured in Thompson's piece, the awe of seeing the gifts nature provides here never really wears off, even for locals.

Island Farming

JESSICA GIGOT

Coming off the ferry, the main road channels you through a small patch of woods before emerging to a collage of farms and farmlettes. On Lopez Island, the entire landscape can appear like one continuous field that fades from a rich Pacific Northwest green into a light tan by the end of July. However, most small farms on the island have their own feel and texture from years of care and tending. Sheep, goats, and cows are scattered throughout, as are marshmallow-shaped bales of hay silage. Copious gardens spill over with luscious vines and bright orange nasturtiums in the summertime.

The San Juan Islands exist in a sun belt, an ideal microclimate that is sunnier and drier than the mainland. Before the Grand Coulee Dam was built in 1942, fruit was a major export of these islands. The creation of dams dramatically increased the irrigated farmland available in central Washington and turned towns like Wenatchee into fruit-growing meccas. According to Historic Barns of the San Juan Islands, "In San Juan County, the Italian prune-plums, which had become very popular through the efforts of the Portland horticulturalist J. R. Cardwell, were first planted on Orcas in the mid-1870s. These were followed by apples and pears, as well as apricots, cherries, peaches, and plums." Despite the industry moving eastward, old stands of trees, now massive and overgrown, remain on several of the islands and still produce a harvest.

In high school, I would come to Lopez to stay at a friend's family cottage. I remember zigzagging from the ferry to their coastal bluff, wondering what it would be like to live full time on an island. We would stay up late watching movies and then venture to the celebrated bakery in town the following morning, groggy and slow. Later, after college, I worked at a summer camp on John's (a remote island that supports a few discreet residences) and would venture over to the larger, more populated islands, like Lopez, on my days off for a dose of their relaxed and calm energy. I idealized this rural haven that had just enough people, not too many and not too few, and a golden glow that stayed with you even as you left on the late-night ferry.

After some exploring in rural Oregon, I found my way back to Lopez Island to work on a family homestead as a farm intern. I wrote about this experience in my memoir, *A Little Bit of Land*; that summer as an island farmer imprinted something special on my young and seeking self. Since that time, many new farms have cropped up throughout the San Juan Islands, offering not only an abundance of products, from vegetables to cheese, but also something more important—food security. To be isolated on an island also means you need to be as self-reliant as possible, able to combat frost and deer damage, in order to have a reliable harvest.

The homestead that I worked on had just about everything—chickens, sheep, a kitchen garden, grain crops, pasture, several fruit trees and berries, and a cow. Milk was plentiful, as one family cow produces quite a bit of volume from its four teats. The farmers, a retired university professor and English teacher, made their own bread and cheese and dedicated a lot of their summer hours to food preservation. I would stare in awe at the multicolored wall of canned food, feeling reverence as if I were peering through the stained-glass window of a church. At this point in my life I was craving tangible skills, a need to connect with nature and feel competent with my hands.

As this was a community-supported agriculture (otherwise known as CSA) farm, several families would come by on a regular basis for a box of vegetables, meat, or a half gallon of milk. These visitors not only brought financial support to the farm, they also created a sense of connection to the rest of the community. A farm can often feel like an island—too many chores and daily responsibilities make it hard to have a normal social life—so it's convenient when people come to you.

As an intern on this farm, I had Sundays off. Some days, I would stay in bed and read. Other times, I would venture into the town center and visit the well-loved red library or ride my bike around the island, coasting over the hills and observing the largely agrarian landscape. The San Juan Islands were once a site for winter villages and seasonal gatherings for several Northern Straits Coast Salish tribes, where they "have tended clam gardens and camas fields, raised wooly dogs, woven baskets and blankets, carved wood and stone, fished, traded, married, died, and held ceremony here for millennia," according to the Island Histories project. The first nonnative settlers arrived in the mid-1850s and began homesteading and farming, which, for better and worse, has shaped the landscape into its current form. Many multigenerational farms persist across the most inhabitable islands, mainly focused on livestock production, but there is also a newer wave of flower, dairy, seed, and vegetables farms that also produce many value-added, farm-based products like jam. At a recent San Juan Islands Agricultural

Summit, 37 percent of attendees were new and beginning farmers, according to the local university extension center.

Most of the San Juan Islands are rocky outcroppings. There are deposits of good, fertile soil, but building up tilth for food production takes a concerted effort. During my summer internship, I worked on creating and maintaining compost piles from garden scraps and animal bedding. It was a practice of transformation, gathering materials and noticing how they changed. Time and temperature melded nitrogen and carbon into fertility that would be reincorporated into garden soils. This process made me more aware of what I used and discarded, and where it eventually ended up. Elation and relief are the best way to describe the satisfaction that comes from creating soil anew from unwanted waste.

Milking a cow every day was a revelation. The arduous repetition was hard to take at first, but then I started to find comfort in the regularity of the routine. Her light brown hide was the same color as the grassy hillsides now faded by summer's aridity. I can't forget the smooth texture of her udder, its humble swell and life-giving warmth. She trotted with enthusiasm into the barn and back out to her luscious pasture in the evening. The milk that filled the stainless steel bucket glowed like a pearl. I was not bold enough to crack a raw egg into a cold glass of raw cow's milk, like the farmer I worked for did, but I experimented with the excess milk in my free time.

In the barn kitchen, next to the sacred wall of preserves, I used the stovetop to heat the milk in a large pot. Stirring continuously, I waited until the milk reached 190 degrees F. Then I turned off the heat and kept stirring as I added a few tablespoons of lemon juice. Soon, the small curds started to appear and float to the top. The milk was coagulating. I poured the curds into a colander lined with muslin cheesecloth and captured the whey in a bowl underneath to feed to the chickens. The separation of whey from curds was alchemy, and I marveled at the vivid yellow liquid, possibly too valuable to feed to poultry. I then hung my bag of fresh curds in the kitchen window, alight with afternoon sun. A few hours later, I had a bright, squeaky cheese that I cut into slices and ate with some of the farm's fresh bread and red-ripened tomatoes. Despite having recently graduated from college, I felt like making my first batch of cheese was my most important accomplishment. I have carried that joy with me into a later chapter as a farmstead cheesemaker.

When I was seven months pregnant with my first daughter, I took a trip to Lopez with my dad and sister. We stayed at an old farmhouse located in what felt like the center of the island. It belongs to a local resident and has been in their family for a long time, but is rented out occasionally. The charming farm kitchen, dining room, and parlor had original wood slat walls that were a step back in time. The kitchen opened to an orchard and large garden. A local farmer rented the land as part of his livestock operation, and we would often see his large truck coming up and down the driveway throughout the day. Land sharing and swapping seemed to be a common island practice. His chestnut-colored horses grazed the field. Lying upstairs in the farmhouse bed, feeling my daughter's fluttering kicks, I imagined what it would have felt like to live and farm here, to raise a family at the turn of the century in the heart of the island with water on all sides. Admittedly, I don't think I could be that brazen, and I imagine that the first female settlers didn't have a choice in the matter.

On a recent trip to San Juan Island—the largest of the archipelago—for a writing residency, I found myself again yearning for island farm life. The irony was that I needed this residency to get perspective on a project that kept getting lost in the folds of busyness in my own farm and family life. It was March and I was working on a new poetry manuscript about ecological grief and early motherhood. Tired of staring at a computer screen, I drove from Friday Harbor to Lime Kiln State Park in hopes of taking in the sunset and maybe seeing a seal or two. It wasn't whale-watching season, but I always hope to see a graceful arc off the cliffy shoreline. The road curved past cattle, a dormant lavender farm almost ready to burst into spring. On a faraway bluff, a flock of Valais blacknose sheep (they look like a stuffie you could grab off a toy store shelf) surrounded a brand new barn and recently cleared field. The newness of that operation was jarring against the island's backdrop of established, multigenerational farms. Worn barns and fence lines, craftsman farmhouses with expansive porches erected on-island in the early 1900s were reliable scenes, along with the foxes that visitors always hope to see.

Last year on Orcas Island, I took some time to venture away from the annual literary festival to visit the lively and eclectic farmers market in Eastsound. It was June and the range of offerings included tacos, ceramics, vegetables, goat cheese, and honey. There is a quiet submission that goes along with farming in place, and farming on an island takes this sense of grounding and identity to a new level. I couldn't help but appreciate the intimacy and sense of celebration that flowed beneath the waves of tourists and locals coming to the market. While I know the hard realities of running a farm, I still find myself admiring the quaintness of the island's sculpted fields and established hedgerows along with the other visitors. Island life seems to amplify the virtues of ruralness in the best of ways.

While production agriculture has its place and history in the San Juan Islands, sustainability and scale were the lessons I carried with me back to the mainland and eventually into my own farm. I no longer live on an island, but my appreciation for the finite resources and space unique to an island have shaped the way I farm and relate to food. I recall the craft and care that went into each day's work. From my time as a farm intern, I went on to study soil and agriculture in graduate school and start my own small sheep creamery. The vague outlines of San Juan, Orcas, and Lopez Islands are visible from my bedroom window across the Salish Sea. I will never forget my taste of island life—surrounded by salt water, hands covered in dirt, nourished by the knowledge that care and community will keep us all from going adrift.

About This Story

This piece by poet, farmer, and writing coach Jessica Gigot, who lives on a small sheep farm in Washington's Skagit Valley, attests to the fact that you don't need to grow up on a farm to end up running one. Wanting to spend some time on an island farm, we initially talked to San Juan Island shepherdess Sarah Pope, who pointed out to us that wool is "a totally sustainable resource. It comes off of an animal that, if it's correctly managed, can be contributing to the health of the land" by cycling nutrients back in.

Despite much of the land on the island being under active management and preserved as viewsheds, Sarah showed us how the soil quality has gone down without attention to regenerative farming methods. "When you just cut hay and cut hay and cut hay, you're taking nutrients out. If you're not using animals to cycle nutrients back in, you're just kind of mining the soil over time. . . . When you don't manage the land—meaning, you're not sort of in active stewardship of it—that's what happens over time. So, part of what we're about here is learning as much as we can about regenerative processes and trying to use the animals in a way that helps to bring back that balance." When not tending to the sheep or land, Sarah produces wool for her company, San Juan Woolworks, and along with her husband helps to run San Juan Islands Food Hub.

Inspired by our time with Sarah, we were eager to find a piece that reflected on island agriculture. Several people enthusiastically recommended the award-winning memoir *A Little Bit of Land* by Jessica Gigot. With a chapter about her time on a homestead on Lopez Island, the book delves into the intricacies of small-scale agriculture in the Pacific Northwest, the changing role of women in a male-dominated industry, and sustainability, economics, and health in the food system. We emailed Jessica to see if she might be interested in writing a piece for us that would give a more complete overview of agriculture on the islands along with her own experience there, and we were delighted when she agreed. We encourage you to pick up *A Little Bit of Land* and consider ways you may be able to support farmers when you visit.

Living High

JUNE BURN

Excerpted from *Living High: An Unconventional Autobiography*

"Our name is Burn," Farrar said to the man in the outer office. "We've come to see about homesteading one of your islands."

Without a word, the man turned and opened a door behind him.

"Here they are!" he yelled, and the whole office force came out to greet us like kinfolks. It was like getting home after a long absence. And we held our breath—they had found our island! Someone had been buying it—the last homestead island in Puget Sound. But Farrar's two years naval service gave him priority rights. They would return the man's payments and we were free to move on and file.

It's just a rock pile, they said. No trees? Oh, plenty of trees. But it was only fifteen acres. Fifteen acres! Why, that was a domain. They said it was so little it didn't show on the map. We looked. Sentinel Island in Speiden Channel—it had a name! And it did show—a sizeable dot. It had a topographical ring on it. It was over a hundred feet high. No water, though. Oh, we'd catch rain water. It rained a lot here, didn't it? No beaches, they said. It wasn't a beach we wanted, it was high, firm seclusion—an eagle's perch from which to survey the world. . . .

• ✦ •

Little by little we were assembling things to take with us. A tent, rented from the company for two dollars a month. A twenty-dollar coupon book for groceries taken against future earnings. On a Saturday afternoon we borrowed the company rowboat, took aboard all our things, and started for Sentinel for the first time.

Farrar was a fine oarsman. Rock-breaking had toughened him. His boyhood on the Arkansas River had prepared him for this.

But not for tides!

When we got outside the harbor and into Speiden Channel beyond Pearl Island, that day, we saw there was a wind. Anyone else would have known it long before, from the movement in the treetops. But we didn't know it. The whitecaps were rolling. They looked formidable. We realized that it was risky to make a crossing in our high-piled shallow boat with the wind blowing against what seemed a strong, contrary current.

"Must be a tide out here," Farrar said wisely. But tides on the open ocean which he had known, are one thing; on enclosed waters, quite another.

We turned back to a little beach on the lee side of our point. And then we did something which Farrar still blushes to think of. We pulled our little boat up onto the beach, tied the painter to a branch of an old alder tree against the bank, and went back to the hotel to wait until next morning.

During the night a wind and a higher tide than usual overturned the boat and emptied its contents all over the beach. Typewriter, trunk, bags, tent were scattered, some of them open, all of them wet. That is what we found the next morning, when, in radiant sunshine, we came running to finish our trip to Sentinel. It looked so bad it tickled us. We hugged each other and laughed.

"You can always expect more than you expect," Farrar said. . . .

• ✦ •

I sat facing Sentinel and watched it leap forward to meet us with every stroke of the oars. When we were nearly there, we crossed a field of hoary grandmother kelp, thirty-foot-long streamers, like gruesome hair, spread out in the tide. The water looked dark and deep, there in the kelp bed. Nine dogfish floated out of it and followed our boat, their hideous faces leering. Small sharks they were. Farrar rowed around the shore till he found a cove where we could pull the boat far up on the rocks—farther than any tide could reach. Thus he still pulls up boats.

Sentinel, the homestead island—at last we stepped onto that bit of earth that was ours. We went over to a clump of trees, trod the long dry grass, looked up at the sky through yellowing maple leaves, some of them a foot across. This was the big leafed maple.

Now we must unload the boat and spread things out to dry. But, look—a long perfect plank! We'll get that first.

Beach wood still seems to me the most wonderful thing in the Puget Sound country. It comes in as new-cut logs, broken from the rafts. It comes as shake bolts which can be split into long satiny shakes to roof your cabin. This white treasure is piled and heaped at the top of every beach on the Sound.

Grass and forest meet on the very top of Sentinel. There we made our first camp site, underneath firs three feet through, the yellowed grass sweeping up over the crest of the hill to their roots. We stood a hundred and twenty-five feet above the water. Vancouver Island, in Canada, lay to the west and smaller Canadian islands were nearer. San Juan, Henry, Pearl, and Battleship Islands spread their pattern of bays and beaches to the south; the Olympic Peninsula across Juan de Fuca, on further. Speiden rose behind us, long and tall. We could see Jones Island to the east and beyond that, the humps of Orcas. The Olympic Mountains were our southern horizon and the single white cone of Mt. Baker marked where the sun would rise.

We gathered feathery fir twigs for a campfire. In the Puget Sound country you can start a fire with one match anywhere and any time, for all its reputation for rain, for even when everything on the ground is sodden, there are always brittle dry twigs hanging on the trees.

We knew nothing of forest fires then. At home, a campfire in the woods was seldom dangerous. Hardwood leaves and twigs are not tinder to catch fire from the suggestion of a spark. It scares me yet to think how easily we might have burned Sentinel to its bedrock that first day.

A campfire lunch of coffee, bacon and eggs, and toast. Not many of our groceries had been ruined by the drenching they had had. The sugar and salt were spoiled, of course, and there was rice running out of melted sacks. But all in all we came out better than we deserved.

After lunch we must hurry to bring up the things. Trip after trip up and down that steep slick hill. Tent, trunk, bags, boxes, our plank. Weary, back-breaking loads. We'd go down the north side, sinking half to our knees in knight's-plume moss. It was like walking in feathers—no, on an innerspring mattress, for it held together and gave some resistance. Then we'd come up the short way again, past yew trees, the kind you make longbows of, tough and red and everlasting. This wood will sink in water.

Past madrona trees, their leaves like the magnolia but sturdier, tougher, the branches hung with scarlet berries, now. The paper-thin bark was peeling off in scrolls. The madrona is Puget Sound's most beautiful and interesting tree, forever green, leaves shedding surreptitiously, the new ones already there, delicate pink blossoms in spring, bright red berries in fall, cinnamon-red outer bark peeling all the time, the under skin a jade green. It will grow on the driest, rockiest bluffs, yet it looks delicate and as though it needed protection.

All afternoon we worked until we were too tired to cook supper. We ate some cheese and soggy bread and went to our bed on the ground—a feather mattress my mother had given us, and dampish comforters.

The bed looked out over the world. The islands had pulled the dark over them and were only purple blurs in the moonlight. Not a single light shone anywhere. The forest hid all the little farms on San Juan Island. The other islands in our range of vision were uninhabited.

Our island. Our world. We had pulled the ladder up and nobody would come. Nobody knew we were here. How tall these trees, their dark crowns brushing the sky! How still it is!

A tugboat rounded Henry Island. Its lights crept up the International Boundary channel. We could hear its engines going in a soft chug-chug. It was a good sound.

The last thing I remembered was Farrar leaning on his elbow, gazing and gazing. And the first thing I saw in the morning was Farrar on his elbow, waiting to show me the morning world with only its fir tips sticking up out of the low mist which hid the water. The world had been down for a swim and was just coming up again. The sun rose over Mt. Baker. The mist sped away. And there was the new day.

"These are the 'days when,'" said Farrar. "We're happy now. This is what it's all about. This is what we were born for. We own the world."

• ✦ •

Sometimes we lost track of time. Once we lost, or gained, a week. It wouldn't have mattered, except that we had to keep track of the tides for our fishing. This time we went out on what we thought was a slack tide. We rowed around Speiden to the north side, up to the bay where the codfish were hanging out those days. When we got there, we found ourselves in the maddest tide rip, and the swiftest ebb we had ever seen. Before we knew what had happened, the thing had grabbed our boat and flung us far out into the channel. We rowed for dear life, barely gaining an inch, zigzagging back toward shore. At last we made it and I got out on shore to pull the boat around the bad spot while Farrar kept it off the rocks with his oar.

My hair had grown long. It came down over my eyes.

My stockings came down over my shoes. The bank was slippery with seaweed and steep, and I had on rubber soles. Hair-blinded, stocking-lamed, nothing but fear kept me from falling into that tide rip. Meanwhile, Farrar was pushing with his oar—he had to stand up in the boat to use force enough to keep it from being dashed onto the shore. Even so, the water boiled over into the boat and the rip jerked it about. It was all he could do to stand up.

It must have taken us an hour to inch our way up that shore and around the dangerous point. At last we gained the comparatively calm water of a little cove at the upper, narrow end of Speiden. And there, on shore, standing in the middle of a potato field, was Dad Chevalier, doubling over with laughter. I was furious, but Farrar laughed, too, and I saw I would be in that hateful woman position of seeming a spoilsport if I lashed out, so I bottled up my anger and sat down in the sun until I could stop trembling. We had come as near to drowning as people can come and live. If I hadn't been born with a caul, we would probably be in Davy Jones's locker right now. . . .

• ✦ •

Along toward Christmas time they began to wonder what Christmas would be like without any money or toys or Christmas dinner. We promised them that with Christmas trees growing at our very door, rose hips and snowberries to make chains, they would remember this as the happiest Christmas of their lives. As a matter of fact, friends sent many gifts for the boys so they would have had something in any case.

On Christmas Eve we took the boys up to the study cabin to spend the night. We built a fire for them and left them tucked up in that solitary place, feeling a little timid, I think, though they wouldn't say so. They were to come down next morning when they heard a whistle. They had a clock so they wouldn't get up too early.

Early next morning Farrar moved the Christmas tree up to the new cabin we had built. We built a huge fire in the fireplace, decorated the cabin with fir and cedar boughs, cones, moss, snowberries, great clusters of madrona berries which lasted, that year, until after New Year. The cabin was beautiful. The bunks were made up, one on each side of the door. We had built the cabin with Eve sides so that the fireplace could be in one corner and still leave the cabin exactly divisible by two.

At seven we whistled for the boys and I went up the trail to meet them, blindfolded them, and led them about the brush for awhile, telling them they were going into a secret cave. At the door of the cabin we got down on hands and knees and crawled into the cave.

We took off their blindfolds when they were seated on their own bench beside the fire.

The boys blinked at the light and color. "It's our cabin," shouted North. "Oh, Bobby, it's a cabin for us! See the bunks!"

It was the happiest Christmas of their lives. . . .

• ✦ •

It had been a fruitful two winters and three summers. A golden age. Salmon leaping below my study bluff, ships from Japan steaming up the International Boundary beyond Skipjack Island, lighthouses throwing their long gleams down the starlit channels. Three log cabins and remembered hours beside their glowing fires, close family togetherness such as we will never know again, I think.

About This Story

We stumbled across June Burn's 1941 memoir, *Living High,* as we were browsing the shelves at the Shaw General Store while waiting in the car line for the ferry. June was described to us by a local as "ahead of her time," but we had no clue how radically unconventional a life she and her husband, Farrar, had lived. In her preface, June writes about the course they set for themselves: "We said we would retire first and enjoy family togetherness as nature intended, giving to our children that more than bread alone by which man lives. We said we would taste life at first hand, dig for our own food, scratch about just anyhow for what we needed, going at it the hard way, letting our children see into the primitive mechanics of living. . . . They and we have had fun, happiness, joy, splendid hardship, fine adventures."

The San Juan Islands today still attract people looking for an unconventional life. We stayed in a cabin at Saltwater Farm on San Juan Island and spoke with owners Merriss Waters and Andrew

Fleming. What started as a dream to have a garden, some goats, and maybe a few weddings became a "snowballed version" when they stepped onto the 10-acre property they now own. Today, Saltwater Farm is a working farm that hosts weddings in the summer and in the offseason hosts cooking events, fundraisers, community events, and retreats, besides renting out the cabins on the property for guests and family reunions. "We believe strongly in bringing community together, spending time in nature with loved ones, and making Saltwater Farm climate positive and sustainable for future generations," they explain.

Marching Orders

ABIGAIL MORGAN PROUT

It has taken 17 years
to move back home
to accept and be accepted by
the island that
made me my own
and to find the bones I buried
in the woods as a girl

A dollop of land, this finite place
everything is recycled, reused
nothing goes to waste
even karma so thick
it's hard to wade through
growing tangled deep
forest of my heart

Rewriting the places that
were soaked in memories
I dodge the familiar forms
in the produce aisle next to me
trying to avoid

coming face to face
with my younger selves

A glass bowl held steady
the history of others in my hands
helping elders to cross
the street who helped me
to cross as a child
together we stand
links in this chain

Lopez called me back
a shrill whistle at recess
to return from the big world
clutching the elixir
of education, experience, heartbreak
back to the roots buried
back to the roots visible

Back to the heartwood
names of my childhood
stack of time's bedrock
building thick sentiment
"When am I?" is the question
waking up different
always in the same place

The workshop of coming home
is path daily chosen
I take my marching orders
from a nursery of tiny raccoons

in a tall bent snag
as they peak their masked faces
from their hollow to listen
I sing to them for hours

Rejoining this waving island tribe
has taken everything I have
and given everything I need
trading anonymous for the fishbowl,
the blank page for the written story,
trading all other mountains
for this single one

Home of Belonging

ABIGAIL MORGAN PROUT

I am building a home of belonging
from repurposed intention
mossy grey pounded shoreline
tall black sway forests
of fir, damp cedar, alder

I belong to the roaring walls
of solstice fires
the ritual yearly witness of
our island children as they cross
the threshold, flower crowned and grown

I belong to the Salish sea,
the teacher of patience as I learn how
to wait for boats
and wait for boats
and wait

I belong to the awe of the tides,
ocean of emotion

twice changing in a day
a reminder of how much
is in constant shift under the surface
in and out and through
the narrow ripping straights
pulling between the craggy channels

I belong to the slicing barnacles,
tight black-lipped mussels,
bright sandpaper sea stars,
each one a party favor for the soul

I belong to deep teal kelp alleyways,
woven with sleek shots of seals
gunning for sockeye
breaking the tension
with loud whelps! of air
to gaze with detachment
towards our land-lubbing ways

I belong to the people that came
before us in the crunch of
clam shells underfoot
joyful reverence, smoke of salmon
sacred in longhouses
sweet scent of hand hewed cedar
singing to the same spirits
that I sang to in the forest
this morning, repurposing intention

I belong to the story
of the Orca whale, Mama Tahlequah,
nosing the sucking currents,
pushing her stillborn calf
around our shale island
for seventeen days without eating,
consumed by grief,
tireless, as if to say,
"See what I have loved and lost.
Do not look away. See this. Feel this."

Just like her,
I belong to what I love
when we love something
with our whole heart,
we belong to it forever

About This Story

We discovered Abigail Morgan Prout's 2021 poetry collection, *Walk Deep,* in the used book room, which is more like a closet, at the Lopez Bookshop on Lopez Island—and it made me, Ilyssa, cry in public twice. Not only does it capture the spirit and reasons for return that we heard from so many boomerang residents—islanders who move away to other cities or parts of the world only to return—but it also reflects upon the tragic story of Tahlequah and her baby. The beloved Southern Resident killer whale gave birth in 2018 to a calf that died soon after, and she carried her baby on her head for seventeen days as she swam a thousand miles, likely from deep grief. Tragedy struck again in early 2025, when Tahlequah was spotted in Puget Sound area carrying the body of another deceased calf—again reminding us not only of the profound bond between mother and calf, but the ongoing challenges killer whales face in this region.

Prout is a native of Lopez Island, where her upbringing "as a wild island hippie child" instilled in her "a profound respect for the natural world" and "the understanding that Nature wasn't just a backdrop for our lives but the sacred text by which we lived." Often as we explore our independence as we enter adulthood, we grapple with the question, *Do I stay or do I go?* Prout writes that "thirty-five years on Lopez have taught me the essence of belonging—to the land, to a community, and to family." She explains that *Walk Deep*, which won a Nautilus Book Award, "calls attention to the power that a familiar outer landscape has as a companion, mirror, compass, and divination tool for our inner landscape."

Writing the Interisland Ferry

IRIS GRAVILLE

Excerpted from *Writer in a Life Vest: Essays from the Salish Sea*

Growing up in Chicago and then smaller cities and tiny towns in the southern parts of Illinois and Indiana, I never imagined I'd someday live on an island in the Salish Sea. In fact, soon after moving from the Midwest to Seattle, I thought my husband's suggestion we visit the San Juan Islands meant a trip to the Caribbean! Yet, after nearly thirty years as an islander, I can't picture myself living anywhere but Lopez Island, one of 419 islands—most of them uninhabited—in the Salish Sea's San Juan Archipelago.

What power draws me to the Salish Sea? It's not just the water's satiny surface on a calm day or the racing white caps when the wind picks up. Part of the attraction is how the color shifts from almost black, to steel gray, to US-flag blue, to, occasionally, the blue-green of the Mediterranean. Surely some of the lure is the way the inland water sweeps driftwood to the shore and swirls around bull kelp and sea grasses. Ebbs and floods soothe me, even as they pick up velocity and volume with tide changes. I'm always astounded by the majesty of pods of orcas gliding and diving in synchrony; or harbor seals' rounded heads, blunt snouts, and brown eyes that pop up at my kayak's stern; or Steller sea lions sunbathing on barnacled rocks.

I attribute my love for the Salish Sea to all these individual features and more. But my true passion is for the way every lovely and fascinating part works with all the others in a latticework of life. Tide pools shelter herring eggs that hatch and feed minke whales. The Salish Sea gifts watershed forests with spawning Pacific salmon such as Chinook, coho, and sockeye—feasts for bears, bald eagles, ravens, and martens. Melting mountain snows glide into rivers which flow into wetlands, empty into bays, and swirl into the sea. The ocean connects to canals and lakes, and rivers on other continents, evaporates into clouds, and is filled by rain from skies around the globe. Some of those waters connect us by ferry and canoe, sailboats and transport vessels, carrying us and our goods, our cars and trucks, rice and coffee beans and, yes, oil.

Over the years, I've learned not just about what I love, but also about the perils that threaten this jewel. If we don't take care of the Salish Sea and all that contributes to it, the interwoven lattice of beauty, wildness, fragility, and relationship will collapse. . . .

· + ·

As an islander, I spend considerable hours on the Salish Sea, sometimes in a kayak, but primarily on the Washington State Ferries (WSF), the largest ferry system in the nation and third largest in the world. The fleet carries nearly twenty-five million people a year through some of the most majestic scenery on Earth.

While ferries are my connection to the mainland, the Interisland route travels among only four islands in the San Juans—Lopez, Shaw, Orcas, and San Juan. Over the years, that circuit has supplied time and space for me to write. During an outing with a friend on the Interisland in the spring of 2017, she recalled blog posts I'd written on the vessel during my twice-weekly commute to neighboring Orcas Island. For five years, I worked there as the school nurse. "One of my favorite blogs of yours," my friend volunteered, "was about riding the ferry." I wouldn't realize until later that her comment had lodged in my mind. . . .

• ✦ •

From August 1, 2018 until August 30, 2019, I served as the Washington State Ferries System's first writer-in-residence on the Interisland ferry (a position I created and proposed to the WSF). A crisp, white, table tent with my name in black lettering and the WSF logo in blue identified me and my role as I rode and wrote on the *MV Tillikum*.

The structure of the residency was simple. I planned to walk, not drive, onto the Interisland ferry on Lopez Island with my laptop, journal, and research materials and then ride, write, and read along the route. There would be no cost to me or the ferry system; the Interisland is the only route in the state system that allows walk-on passengers to ride free.

Although I hoped to interview crew members and passengers, I expected to devote most of my time to solitary writing and reading, with the goal of producing a collection of essays focused on protecting and preserving the water and life that surrounded my home. And there would be plenty of time; another anomaly of this route is that walk-on passengers can ride from around six in the morning until eight at night (or later depending on the season) without ever disembarking until the vessel docks for the night at Friday Harbor on San Juan Island.

It took far longer than one term to complete the collection, *Writer in a Life Vest: Essays from the Salish Sea*, but many pieces had their beginnings at a table on the *MV Tillikum*, floating (sometimes pitching port to starboard) past rocky shorelines; snowy mountain ridges; forests of cedars, firs, and madrones; mansions and mobile homes. Seagull and eagle calls, briny wind currents, and tingling sea breezes stimulated my senses.

Friends And Relatives

Most passengers just refer to it as "the ferry." They know where it's headed, what time it departs the ferry terminal, and when it arrives at its destination. The name of the vessel isn't clearly listed on the WSF's online ferry schedule. If you look closely when you board, though, you'll find a small, wooden sign somewhere near the ferry's wheelhouse with the vessel's name carved on it. And some people take that name very seriously.

Washington State Ferries (WSF) are considered part of the state's highway network; the fleet of twenty-one vessels serves eight Washington counties as well as British Columbia, Canada. It's the Washington State Transportation Commission's (WSC) responsibility to name these vessels as well as state highways and bridges. For ferries, state guidelines require the names have "statewide significance and represent Washington's image and culture," while avoiding "commercial overtones and anything offensive." Names of tribes, bodies of water, geographic locations, or terms that relate to nautical heritage meet those requirements. . . .

The Coast Salish people have lived on and cared for these lands and waters since time immemorial, making Coast Salish words the language of the Salish Sea. So it's fitting that now, with the exception of the *MV Rhododendron*, all current WSF vessels have tribal names. They include:

Tillikum, Chinook jargon with elements from Chinook, Nootka, English, French, and other languages that means "friends and relatives."
Chelan from the Wenatchi word *tsillan* for "deep water."
Sealth for Suquamish and Duwamish Chief Sealth, after whom the City of Seattle was named.
Tokitae, Coast Salish dialect for "nice day, pretty colors."
Kittitas, the tribe of "shoal people" who lived along the shallow portion of the Yakima River near Ellensburg, also defined as "land of bread."

WSF Song

"But did he ever return? No, he never returned
And his fate is still unlearned
He may ride forever 'neath the streets of Boston
He's the man who never returned
—Jacqueline Steiner and Bess Lomax Hawes, "MTA Song"

The "MTA Song" appeared in 1956 as a campaign song for the Progressive Party candidate for mayor of Boston. A version of it became a 1959 hit when recorded by American folk-singing group the Kingston Trio. The song inspired me to write this parody when a winter freeze almost made me "the writer who never returned"...

Well, let me tell you a story 'bout a writer named Iris
Who boarded the ferry one wintry morn.
She wrote and she wrote until the third island stop
When she started to feel a bit worn.

Will she ever return? Oh, will she ever return?
For her Lopez home she'll yearn.
She may ride forever round the San Juan Islands,
The writer who never returned.

She didn't pay a fare, walking on and off is free,
And she could ride and write all day,
But at San Juan Island she was feeling pretty hungry,
So, she trudged to the Bean Café.

Will she ever return? Oh, will she ever return?
For her Lopez home she'll yearn.
She may ride forever round the San Juan Islands,
The writer who never returned.

A waiter told the writer, while she lunched at the Bean,
"Ice has frozen the Lopez dock!"
Then the writer's heart skipped several beats
As she felt a wave of shock.

Will she ever return? Oh, will she ever return?
For her Lopez home she'll yearn.
She may ride forever round the San Juan Islands,
The writer who never returned.

The Washington State Ferries sent an email alert
That repairs would likely take all night,
So, Iris called some friends on San Juan Island,
The kind souls prepared a bed and bite.

Will she ever return? Oh, will she ever return?
For her Lopez home she'll yearn.
She may ride forever round the San Juan Islands,
The writer who never returned.

A midnight alert said the Lopez dock was working,
and a ferry would be coming right by.
So, her friends drove her to the boat
and she let out a grateful sigh.

Will she ever return? Oh, will she ever return?
For her Lopez home she'll yearn.
She may ride forever round the San Juan Islands,
The writer who never returned.

Now you island dwellers who travel by ferry,
Don't forget you must come prepared.
Pack a toothbrush and chargers for all your devices
In case your vessel becomes impaired.

Will she ever return? Oh, will she ever return?
For her Lopez home she'll yearn.
She may ride forever round the San Juan Islands,
The writer who never returned.

One week later, snowfall covered the islands
But the ferries continued to churn.
Iris took another chance as Writer-in-Residence.
She's the writer who always returns.

Will she ever return? Oh, will she ever return?
For her Lopez home she'll yearn.
She may ride forever round the San Juan Islands
The writer who never returned.

About This Story

Ferries are an essential part of the island experience, so we knew this collection wouldn't be complete without a story that focused solely on the experience of traveling on one—or waiting for one. As we read in Abigail Prout's poem "Home of Belonging," one facet of living on the island is waiting and waiting for boats. Ferries are so much a part of life that locals have learned to have a sense of humor about it—and to show up early for the car line—and tourists who haven't yet learned the patience required for riding the ferry practically throw their wallets at souvenir shops to buy "WTF: Where's the Ferry?" shirts.

Fittingly, we picked up Iris Graville's book *Writer in a Life Vest* just before hopping on the interisland ferry and gave the essays a read while riding between destinations. Iris got her start writing on the ferry during her five years commuting to Orcas Island, where she wrote most of her 2017 memoir, *Hiking Naked: A Quaker Woman's Search for Balance.* In addition to praise from her friend for her blog posts on riding the ferry, Iris credits her inspiration to write this collection of essays to a growing concern about climate change and the health of the Salish Sea, compromised by threats to the orcas, reduction of the salmon population, sea star wasting, endangerment of birds and mammals, and the risk of spills from increased oil transit. Her "WSF Song" we thought could be a good campfire song or sea shanty for our dear readers to keep themselves entertained while waiting for the next ferry.

Shared Waters, Shared Home

LYNDA V. MAPES

Excerpted from *Orca: Shared Waters, Shared Home*

The *Tyrannosaurus rex* of the sea, orcas worldwide are devastating predators, ready to rip their prey with a mouthful of conical interlocking teeth. Ruthless, precision carnivores, orcas live up to their species name, *Orcinus orca*, "from the realm of the dead." They get their kill, whatever it is, wherever it is, whatever it takes. Globally, orcas target about 140 species—stingrays, sharks, sea lions, herring, minke whales, baby gray whales, octopi, and much, much more. Their teeth reveal their obsessions. Shark killers' teeth become worn down from taking on rough-skinned prey. Chinook shredders have teeth sharp enough to tear big fish in half with a shake of their head.

With the orcas' cunning intelligence, formidable power, and martial-art moves, no animal on their menu is safe. In Australia, orcas thrash their tails to karate-chop great white sharks and rip their livers out. Orcas chase down, ram, and drown baby gray whales off the coast of California and tear off their lips and tongues. They storm the beaches of Patagonia and snatch baby southern sea lions and southern elephant seals right off the sand.

They body-slam and hurl white-sided dolphins through the air in the Salish Sea and herd herring in Norway into terrorized silvery torrents, the better to clobber them with their tails to stun them, then gulp them by the thousands.

In the Antarctic, orcas slash through the water, fast and powerful as packs of wolves. They work together to make waves that wash seals right off the ice, straight into their jaws. Orcas swim bluefin tuna to death in the Strait of Gibraltar, attacking them as they enter and exit the Mediterranean Sea during their breeding migration. Orcas chase the fast-swimming fish for forty minutes at a time, until the tuna are exhausted, then close in for the kill. Alaskan resident orcas have learned to respond to the sound of a fisherman's hydraulic winch sure as a dinner bell, swarming in at the sound of the gear being raised to quickly pick luscious, freshly caught black cod right off the hooks.

The largest species of dolphin (a toothed whale), orcas are—while not abundant in numbers—the most widely distributed mammals on Earth, other than humans. Orcas dominate the food web in every ocean, from the pack ice edges in the Northern and Southern Hemispheres to the equatorial tropics.

Orcas easily swim 75 miles a day, with bursts of speed up to 30 miles an hour. They are big animals: males are typically up to 26 feet long and weigh as much as 12,000 pounds; females are smaller at about 23 feet long and 6,000 pounds. Males can sprout a dorsal fin 6 feet tall at sexual maturity.

They have one of the largest brains of any mammal other than humans and some of the areas of their brains are larger and more complex than our own, particularly the parts that support empathy and social interaction. This explains a lot. Whenever people say to me, "They are just like us," the first thing that flashes through my mind is, *Don't flatter yourself.*

It is their intelligence and culture that truly set orcas apart from all other mammals, humans included. Whether measured in family loyalty, intergenerational support, or diplomacy, orcas are the superior species. For one thing, they are far and away our elders: In their modern form, orcas have been on this earth for some six million years. While there is only one species of orca, they have evolved into multiple populations across the planet. These are societies of great antiquity, each with its own culture, learned and passed on through generations. . . .

Summer Splendor in the Salish Sea

The southern resident orcas' summer home has been the Salish Sea for some ten thousand years. It is a place of enchantment, a world of glissading motion, swirling blue and green water, and soft sounds. Out exploring on a midsummer day in 2018, Joe Gaydos, science director of the nonprofit SeaDoc Society, slowed the society's research vessel, the *Molly B*, as we passed by the rocky shore of an uninhabited island. It was just a dot in the San Juan Islands, one of more than 172 islands and reefs, many without even a name, located in the Salish Sea west of Anacortes in Skagit County, Washington. I heard a chorus of quiet peeping.

"Pigeon guillemots," Gaydos said, as the young chicks made soft, high sounds. They were calling to their parents as the adults returned to their nests. Nearby, oystercatchers patrolled the rocks, waggling their brilliant long red beaks, a jaunty contrast with their jet-black feathers. The water was glassy, the sun a golden beneficence. Mount Baker towered supreme over the land and water, more than ten times as high at its glaciered peak as the depth of Puget Sound's darkest abyss. Tidal currents churned and whirled as Gaydos piloted the boat slowly and quietly past more uninhabited islands, tufted with firs and aglow with the brick-red trunks of madronas.

Harbor seals lounged, perhaps sleeping off a meal. Masters of the deep dive, they can plunge to 1,600 feet and stay submerged more than half an hour. They fish by feel, with whiskers ten times more sensitive than a rat's, enabling them to detect undulations caused by the movement of a fish in the water. "They can sense the hydrodynamic track of the fish thirty seconds after it passes," Gaydos said. With their mottled coats, the sleeping seals looked as immobile and inert as the rocks they slept on, hiding in plain sight as they basked. A salmon leapt from the blue, flashing silver-bright, then disappeared into the depths.

Glacier-carved, the Salish Sea is more than 2,000 feet deep in its deepest fjords and straits, but it also shallows to bays and sills, nearshore beaches and sloughs, mudflats and salt marshes, eelgrass meadows and kelp beds. These varied homes nurture thousands of marine species, from whales and seals and salmon to lingcod and rockfish, crabs and clams. In all, about 37 species of mammals, 172 species of birds, 253 species of fish, and more than 3,000 species of invertebrates make their home in the Salish Sea, according to the SeaDoc Society, including some of the world's oldest and largest animals of their kind: Pacific giant octopus and the world's largest barnacle, chiton, sculpin, anemone, and jellyfish. Some Puget Sound rockfish live more than a century, and red urchins abide as long as 150 years. The world's oldest orca was believed to have been southern resident orca J2. She may have been close to one hundred years old when she died in 2016.

Gaydos and I watched as seal pups, just born in the summer height of the pupping season, nursed at the soft curve of their mothers' bellies, eyes half-closed in sleepy delight. The quick arch of a harbor porpoise breaking the water's surface punctuated the haze clinging to the blue shine of the water. The porpoise rose and dove, the chuffing of its breath carrying a long way in the quiet. A black, orange, and white rhinoceros auklet hurled its chunky seabird body through the air as if thrown rather than flying. Harlequin ducks ran noisily across the sea, feet slapping the water as they raced for liftoff, the current swirling in whirlpools.

Seals wise to our boat slipped into the water without a splash, their young inching urgently after them. Clumsy on the rocks, they were all liquid grace once they hit the water. The rocks were wreathed with clean, fresh green algae and bronze kelp, and the air had a tangy, briny scent as the tide raised its voice, rushing up the shoreline.

Gaydos turned off the engine and we drifted, the sunshine warm on our backs even as a cool sea breeze came off the water. We started unpacking lunch and talked about all we had seen that morning—including the stark black pinnacles of orca dorsal fins, off in the distance. These highly intelligent, socially sophisticated orca families have undeniable charisma and presence. Some scientists don't like to talk about culture in wildlife, because it sounds like anthropomorphism, Gaydos said, referring to inappropriately attributing human characteristics to the behavior of nonhuman animals. But the southern resident orcas have what humans call culture: learned behavior, passed on intergenerationally, including language, ceremonies, hunting and gathering skills, usual and accustomed gathering and hunting spots, and distinct food preferences.

Cultural Bonds

So much of what resident orcas do is passed on by social learning, said John K. B. Ford, a renowned Canadian orca expert. Beginning in 1977, he was among the first to decipher the calls of resident orcas and understand their importance. Ford discovered there was nothing random about these calls, but rather, they were organized in dialects, taught and learned—a rare thing in the animal kingdom. The ability to learn and repeat sounds is unique to a very small group of animals, just one more way in which resident orcas are so unusual, Ford told me, sharing the thrill of some of those first years of discovery.

"It was a really exciting time; things started falling into place as we began to understand the structure of their society," Ford said. "They are one of the most advanced societies and cultures in the nonhuman world. They are a very special animal; with their dialect structure and acoustic repertoires, they are culturally unique. These dialects have persisted probably for centuries."

The most characteristic signals of orcas around the world are pulsed calls, of about one to two seconds. These are loud calls, audible in quiet conditions farther than 10 miles away. The three ecotypes of orcas—residents, transients, and offshore—produce sounds that are distinct. No orca from any of these different types would mistake who they were hearing.

In addition to calls they share, the resident orca pods each also have calls unique to them. These calls allow family members to travel together in a vast, dark ocean. They are seldom separated by more than a few miles or hours.

Like the orcas, the Lummi people never stayed fixed in a single place. Regular seasonal migration routes to fishing sites, berry and other harvesting grounds, hunting sites for game and waterfowl, and winter villages encompassed a large territory, sometimes overlapping with other Native American tribes and First Nation bands. The ancestors of the present-day Lummi people occupied much of the San Juan Islands, as well as coastal lands from as far north as British Columbia's Fraser River to as far south as the environs of Seattle.

Coast Salish native people have long respected orcas and never hunted them. They see in their lifeways many of their own family traditions, said the late Tsi'li'xw Bill James, hereditary chief of the Lummi people, whose reservation today is located near Bellingham, in Whatcom County, Washington.

Spring rain fell softly, the woodstove ticking with heat as James sat in his favorite chair by the picture window framing a big fir where eagles often roost. His home looked out to the salt water of Puget Sound, toward Lummi Island. I wasn't at all surprised to find students working by the woodstove when I dropped by James's house on the reservation; he was a generous teacher. The students were softening strips of cedar bark to fashion a thick tassel for a woven-cedar chief's hat, traditional regalia of the Coast Salish people.

His mother, the late Fran James, taught him, "Keep your hands busy," and her knitting needles rested on a side table next to his chair. The carved-yew needles, passed down to her from her mother, were polished from years of use. Her homemade spinning wheel, fashioned from scavenged parts, still stood in the workroom curtained off from the sitting room.

The floor was heaped with cedar bark ready for weaving and fragrant, fresh cedar shavings from carving. Baskets and hats in various stages of completion surrounded James, and I knew if I asked, he would bring out the suitcases to show me recently completed handwoven wool blankets and shawls. James was a master weaver, and his work as well as his mother's is cherished by collectors and hanging in museums all over the region.

The quiet, rhythmic thud as two students pounded cedar bark punctuated James's sentences as he began sharing the story of how the orcas, also called blackfish, came to be known by his people as family.

"An elder told me the story of the blackfish and how important it is that we remember who we are and where we come from and what they mean to us," James said. "The Changer that made the human beings also changed humans to animals, and in this way all living things in the Lummi understanding are related. That is how we have to show our respect to all the things that were created from the human beings. We remember, we give thanks to all the things we eat, that we gather. We give thanks because we know they came from our people at one time."

"This is just a glimpse of how we believe," James said. "There are many stories of the people that live under the water, under the ice, the star people—they are all related to us. I know lots of stories, lots of the history that I carry within me. The blackfish are called *qwel lhol mech ten*: 'the people that live under the sea'. . . . There are many, many creation stories. They were told by our people about who we are and where we come from. We have to share these so our young ones know."

About This Story

The Seattle Times environmental journalist Lynda V. Mapes calls herself "an explorer and reveler in the natural world" and explains that she's "driven to go deep, look long, stay awhile." Since her book *Orca: Shared Waters, Shared Home* was published in 2021, scientists have suggested a reclassification of resident and transient killer whales as two *distinct* species instead of two groups within a single species. And, to make matters more complex, the naturalist on our whale-watching tour shared that there are other ecotypes of killer whales that may also end up being their own species.

These differences had been suspected for decades, but the recommendations were announced just days before our trip to the islands. This made it an exciting time to find ourselves on the water looking for these creatures. While these distinctions may seem trivial, better understanding can result in better protection for the various orcas *and* their biodiverse habitats. Actions informed by science—such as tailored conservation strategies, population monitoring, and protective laws and regulations—can help.

The Child's Song

MICHAEL DALEY

The sun goes down over the Strait of Juan de Fuca
and drapes a cool shadow over the trees,
cedar and fir and some coastal yew and madrona.
So many tall trunks,
and then squat curved ones with peeling bark
dangle over the bluff.
Painful to let the sun into your eyes, squinting west
across the blue body of waves,
the border between care and woe.

And then night with its thunder on the rocky beach
two hundred feet below a twisting trail of sand
and wild strawberry, and, carefully off the path,
Indian Paintbrush, orange and black.

Down there a seal is slapping the body of a salmon
against a boulder fallen from a vanished glacial peak.

And the sky goes to stars, their Milk filling the body of the Bear
and spilling onto the trees themselves
down the silver bark of hundreds

of cedar. Like silk, ever so lightly,
the moths driven from moist sod,
moonlight unfolds upon the shapeless sea
a shimmering swath across the waves
where we must go, or think we will,
holding our elbows and staring
out from the boughs of the forest.

About This Story

Michael Daley is a retired high school English teacher, poet, creative nonfiction writer, and founding editor of Empty Bowl Press. We learned about Michael's work at Pelican Bay Books and Coffeehouse in Anacortes, Washington, where he lives and cocurates a regular poetry reading series. We were immediately drawn to how his poem, originally published in *Moonlight in the Redemptive Forest*, captures the natural landscape of the islands, particularly the native trees that contrast with the blues of the ocean and the grays of the rocky coastline.

Also known as madrones or strawberry trees, madronas are among the most iconic and common trees of the San Juan Islands. Their cinnamon-red bark peels off in sheets and can glow like embers in the right light on dry rocky bluffs all along the islands. As the bark peels, it reveals hints of yellow and lime green beneath, creating a spectacular array of colors. The trees keep their leaves year-round and produce flowers in the spring and red berries in the fall. We found ourselves constantly pointing out and snapping pictures of them, each with its own personality and configuration of bent limbs that looked almost human at times. More than once their branches or trunks made us giggle uncomfortably, as if we had stumbled upon a stranger's naked body.

San Juans for the Weekend

QUINCY HENRY, AKA Q DOT
Original song

8AM, it's already hectic, wild, and fast paced
Nice guys finish, but is it always in last place?
Stress on my plate, like California's upper crest
Stress on me as tight as a Patagonia puffer vest
Need that release, need peace, I'm needing nothing less
Gesundheit, need to stop everything to resume life
Need to get to back to where it started for she and me
Where near a tree, next to a pond at this Airbnb
We'd seen the sea was deep as our bond, now we are "we"
Sacred as the land we are on
. . . San Juans

3PM, I'm wading in water via the ferry boat
Leave the world behind, it reminds me that there is hope
Friday Harbor, wife and the kids? Very dope
Senses stimulated, invigorated, see through a periscope
The world had me thinking concrete and masonry was made
  for me

Systematically displacing me, distastefully
But hastily, I'm running to view spots
Where hemlocks and dew drops
Move with the wind
Smooth as the moves of the waves
As they do it again
Who could behave as depraved
As they move from within

Somewhere between meditation and hypnosis
The bird feeders and red cedars that sit on Lopez
Between the trails they seem untouched
That's where hope lives
Go beyond what you own, that's what hope gives
Hope I can bring my people to a place they recognize
That what this world made for us could leave us dead inside
But somewhere in the trees, there's good earth to stand on
That place will always and forever be
. . . San Juans

All those who wander are not lost
I seek to be seen here and seek not to be sought
This is how it should be (life)
This is how it could be (life)
This is how, this is how this place reassured me—
It's the magic of Brigadoon in a living room
It's the sighting of orcas while on Orcas
It's quintessential simplistic,
It's naturalistic, natural mystic
No straight lines in nature, what is a misfit?
Homegrown jam on a biscuit

Coffee at dawn
The best things are free and freeing where I belong

8AM, it's easy moving at my pace
I can feel all the tension removed from my space
From my being
3PM, and I'm steady feeling the new balance
Having to leave is the new challenge
The sunsets through the strait
Indescribable and really if you relate
No more survivor mode I need this to replicate
Into everything I go on
. . . San Juans

Mourning the past mornings at Moran
Calls from Cascade Falls alluring
Memories all enduring
AM at Doe Bay, coffee is pouring
Osprey overhead soaring
Feet touch the original wood flooring
This is a come up
Watch the sun come up
It has a different meaning
When you on Mt Constitution leaning
It's easy to lean in
See the horizon without binocular eyes then
Realizing through it all there is a God,
Dogs running like the Iditarod,
Pizzeria Portofino and citronella pods,
And is it odd?
To balance it all out to even

Alive and breathing
. . . the San Juans for the weekend

About This Story

Quincy Henry, a Grammy-nominated rapper and marketing professional, and his wife, Whitni Henry, a former Army combat medic, are the cofounders of Campfire Coffee, a small Black-owned coffee roaster with several shops in Tacoma, Washington, that roasts its beans—yes, you guessed it—over an open fire. To them, their business is about more than just the coffee; it's about building an inclusive outdoor community—a big part of what led us from Instagram friends to fast real-life friends when we finally met following our trip to the San Juan Islands.

As a family that loves to camp together, the Henrys would often reflect on the loneliness of being the only Black family on camping trips. Their outdoors-themed coffee shop inspires people to get outdoors, with a wall of their customers' images on hikes hanging below a sign that reads "Share the Outdoors." They recognize one of the biggest barriers to getting outdoors is the cost, so they founded the Campfire Explorers Club, a nonprofit providing funding to local outdoor education and youth organizations, fully-funded camping trips for local families, a reading library with outdoor-themed books, and a supply of gear to rent or give to those who don't have it.

Our introduction to Quincy was through a friend who invited him to speak at a conference for outdoors professionals, where he received a standing ovation for his talk on using hip-hop to connect people to the outdoors. At our book signing at Campfire Coffee hosted by Grit City Books, we got to talking to Quincy and heard about his short weekend trips to the San Juan Islands with his wife. One thing led to the next, and here we have what goes down in history as the first hip-hop song in our *Campfire Stories* series—and possibly the first hip-hop song about the San Juan Islands. While Quincy's medium is unique, his experience is shared by many, as the islands are a favorite destination for Pacific Northwest residents during the summer months. If you get there, why not let your guard down, find a beat, and give this verse a try?

Lime Kiln

JEREMY VOIGT

We watched the pod pass at Lime Kiln point,
standing together, a family of five, as an otter
emerged and remained fixed on the waterline;

his eyes not towards the milling people in the park,
but eying those larger black and white bodies
making their ponderous way north, mostly invisible,

but the machines tracking their movements told
the Ranger who told us to stay, so we stayed.
They came, with a few boats behind, everything else

out of the way, like the otter flapping his paws
quietly in the water, watching. The black fins
rising straight up, sinking, like a machine needle,

or exclamation points, and I thought of Merwin's
extinction poem, *one must always pretend something
among the dying*, and have always thought thus

one must always pretend, though under summer skies
today, and high clouds there is nothing staged
in the otter's caution, in the breaths from the sea–

relief, shock, awe, or all three, percussive as they came.
Then gone, they were gone. And the otter. Though
we know where they are, like stars turning back to stone.

And of the mother carrying her still born the captain
said, "it's almost human," but after seventeen days
every parent knows, that's the most animal in us all.

About This Story

Our conversations with locals quickly revealed their preference that visitors who come for whale watching observe these already endangered creatures by land—as poet Jeremy Voigt and his family did—rather than water, to ensure their safety and minimize disturbances. Lime Kiln Point State Park on the west side of San Juan Island is one of the best places in the world for this. The park is named for its decades-long history of lime operations, which severely impacted this rocky coastline beginning in 1860, as workers blasted the earth to extract limestone and cut down forests for wood to fuel the kilns that turned the stone into lime that was shipped to customers throughout the region.

The park owes its exquisite whale watching to its position along the Haro Strait, the deepest channel in the San Juan Islands, and the fact that the sea floor drops steeply just offshore, allowing these massive mammals to swim close while feeding. Here, you're likely to encounter orcas, harbor porpoises, sea lions, and seals hunting for fish in the bull kelp forests close to shore. Other wildlife you might spot here includes minke whales, humpback and gray whales, Dall's porpoises, Pacific white-sided dolphins, and river otters.

In his poem, Voigt references W. S. Merwin's 1967 poem "For a Coming Extinction," which is addressed to a gray whale and laments both the environmental destruction that threatens countless other species and the human impulse to look away from the harsh truth of our impact. The somber ending of Voigt's poem reflects upon the story of Tahlequah, also mentioned in Abigail Morgan Prout's poem "Home of Belonging," and the grief every parent can understand.

Island Potluck

SAMUEL GREEN

You might think we go
to the North Bay beach
or the one-room school,
or the edge of the field
near the May pole
for the food, & we do
have an appetite for goat
meat curry, salmon grilled
over alder, tender greens
thinned from a garden
& rinsed in well water,
an old hen stewed in vinegar
on the back of a wood-fired range,
potatoes roasted with rosemary,
baked ling cod, boiled crab
for the cracking, homemade bread
with handmade cheese,
canning jars of cider, jugs
of blackberry wine. Or
we could be there for the music,

the neighbors who pull out
a fiddle, flute, penny whistle,
concertina, bass, guitar. Of course
we go for stories about the old ones
whose names flare at the edge
of conversation like sparks
rising from a campfire: Chuck,
Elaine, Jimmy, Mildred,
Ann. We all miss Dorothy's
deviled eggs. We come to find out
who's well, who's failing, who's falling
in or out of love, for what the young
in the shadows might learn
from their elders, quiet voices
in the driftwood, at the clearing's
edge, out by the school
swings. We bring bowls & serving
spoons, favorite pots & skillets,
a colorful sorting of plates,
& the empty cups of ourselves.

Into the Territory

SAMUEL GREEN

Our son's bedroom resembles a giant kitchen table with six-foot legs. Sally and I are short, so we walk beneath it with ease. Visitors need to bend. Really, it's only two sheets of plywood tacked onto a frame, with four-by-fours for legs and a wooden ladder nailed to one side. Lonnie is eight, and he scampers up the rungs like a chipmunk to a foam pad nest surrounded by toys and baskets of clothes.

The bedroom fills the middle section of the surplus army tent in which we now live. Under his floor are book shelves, and the futon his mother and I roll out each night. The main floor is also made of plywood: twelve sheets squared on a frame set on top of a series of cedar logs dragged from the woods. Each evening, after the futon is made up for bed, Lonnie sprawls across it, loose-limbed, listening to me read from *Huckleberry Finn.* I sit in a rocking chair fashioned from tree limbs, leaning toward the warm, yellow light of a kerosene lamp, book held open in my left hand. Sally rocks in a second chair near another lamp, darning socks, sewing patches on the knees of dungarees, crocheting. Her small hands seem always to be full of one sort of work or another, like little birds that can't stay still. Occasionally she rises to tend the fire in our kitchen range, a Round Oak made in the 'twenties, or to stir a pot of goat stew simmering on a trivet farthest away from the fire box. At the other end of the tent, there's a barrel stove I made from a kit. The two fires make enough heat to bully the late October chill into the farthest corners. The good smell of wood smoke never entirely leaves.

It is 1982. Only a few months ago we lived in a comfortable cinder block home in north Seattle, commuting to jobs in the city while our son lingered in daycare and school. It wasn't what we wanted. We dreamed of a life that would keep us together full time, allow us to write poems, make books, learn what it meant to own ourselves. So we sold our house and everything electric, and moved onto ten acres of logged-over land in the middle of a tiny island, about a hundred miles north. It's an island without many conveniences: no sewer system, no public water, no electricity, no telephones, no stores. A post office offers mail three days a week (if the weather is good), and a tiny school a mile away serves the first eight grades. The only way on or off is by private boat or air taxi. We are roughly in the center. Two miles in any direction, and we wade into cold water. Though we can't know it, we will live in the tent for three years, while I build a log house.

We have no television, and can't yet afford batteries for a radio, let alone a radio itself. Instead, there are books. We've already read *Tom Sawyer* out loud. In the year to come, we'll read the whole *Swallows & Amazons* series, *The Hobbit, The Lord of the Rings*. Lonnie never gets tired of listening. He stretches out on his stomach across the futon, chin resting in the heels of his palms, watching the way my lips move, the gestures of my right hand, how my body shifts back and forth in the rocker. Or he lies on his side, one ear turned to the tight, green canvas roof, letting words fall into his ears like nickels pitched into cups at a carnival. We read for an hour or two every night. When we get to a stopping place, he is filled with dismay: *Just one more page, please, please, pretty-pretty please*! It will be this impatience that will finally push him into reading for himself. Some kids become so hungry for story they will jump into the roughest current of language and flail bravely until they learn how to stay afloat, the way Lonnie and his classmates have learned to roll over kayaks and canoes in one of the small ponds, so they can go safely on field trips to other islands.

Living as we do, it isn't hard to imagine Huck and Jim on the raft, floating lazily under a southern sun, fishing lines dangled over the side. When he takes his pole to the county dock, Lonnie keeps one flap on his overalls loose, the way he imagines Huck might, and goes barefoot until the cold finally chases him into shoes.

In our first months, both Lonnie and Sally sleep soundly, but I lie awake, listening through the thin membrane of canvas: raindrops falling on the waxy leaves of Oregon grape; rats rummaging through branches of ocean spray; the occasional scream of a rabbit dying in a rush of feathers and fur. We can follow a low flock of geese for miles. If a neighbor is up late, driving on the narrow gravel roads, we know whose car it is by the sound of the engine. There are few secrets in this small place. Sometimes Lonnie tries to postpone bedtime by asking for one of the poems my father taught me. *Do it with a voice, Dad.*

And we'll have Peter Lorre doing "The Shooting of Dan McGrew":

"A bunch of the boys were whooping it up, in the Malamute Saloon."

Or James Mason intoning "The Cremation of Sam McGee":

"Now Sam McGee was from Tennessee, where the cotton blooms and blows."

I know these old poems by heart, and it isn't long before my son begins mouthing the words with me, grinning like an otter at his favorite lines.

When fall storms begin, like elephants lined up trunk to tail offshore, waiting for their turn in the ring, I get up several times a night with a flashlight and search for leaks, or for some sign the tent is about to collapse around us. But when the strongest gusts come bucking down the shoulder of the mountain, like a logging truck without brakes, the tent walls simply push in and out, gently. It's like living in a giant lung. Even on still nights I am unsettled, so I get up, untie the tent flaps and step outside to see frost clamped to the ground, the moon like a brooch on a black shawl, Orion stalking the sky above the clearing. It's hard to believe we haven't made a mistake, that we aren't going to have to pay a hard price for happiness.

Each morning we ask Lonnie how he slept. Fine, he says. Did you dream? He tells us:

> I was a barnacle that got tired of its rock.
> *What did you do?*
> Let go, and went to find another.
> *Were you afraid?*
> No.
> *Were you sad to leave your friends?*
> There are lots of barnacles. I was just looking for a rock that wanted me.

His imagination can be risky. When we were building our tent platform, we slept on an old logging road. Lonnie complained of the "ripply" ground beneath his sleeping bag. I told him those were Caterpillar tracks. He spent the long night with visions of hairy giants wriggling through our camp to crush us all. Another time I woke to find he'd joined us on the futon, his head pressed to Sally's chest. When he saw me watching, he whispered: *I was afraid her heart might stop. You know, the way the frogs quit singing, sometimes.* It takes months to realize most of his dreams have to do with life-change, and risk.

The ritual of reading helps him think in terms of narrative. Each day, when he comes bursting through the tent flap, he tells how many seals he saw near the dock, how many white-headed eagles perched on the dead limbs of snags above the beach. Like Twain, he's a good observer, and has a heart as open as the eyes of an owl.

Tom's elaborate plans to rescue Jim from the shed make perfect sense to Lonnie. It doesn't occur to him that we haul water because we don't yet have the money to drill our own well; in his mind, pulling a garden cart full of buckets nearly a mile from a neighbor's well simply makes a better yarn, draws it out, adds flavor. He likes drinking from the tin dipper that hangs above the bucket just outside the back door.

He tells spontaneous stories of his own:

> *Was a whale, wanted to turn into a big, floating tree.*
> *Why?*
> So birds would have some place to land when they got tired.

When I imitate him, he gets impatient:

> *Was a boy who wanted to be a bear.*
> *No!* Was a *bear,* who wanted to be a *boy.*

We begin to add our own adventures to island lore: an otter steals a bag of fish after we leave it on the steps of the post office for only a few minutes; a tiny screech owl gets into our chicken coop and kills a chick, but then clings, terrified, to the wire screen as the broody hen charges back and forth in a hurricane of feathers. We have to rescue it. I think of Robert Frost a good deal in these days, his lines about the land being ours before we were the land's.

We come to the famous end of *Huck Finn*: "I reckon I got to light out for the territory ahead of the rest, because Aunt Sally, she's going to adopt me, civilize me, and I can't stand it. I've been there before."

I hate to close the book. It stays open on my lap. Lonnie is silent for a time, then asks, *Are we in the territory?* His question startles us. Of course we are. Why haven't we noticed? We, too, have slid off the current of the river in order to avoid someone else's idea of how we are supposed to live, and headed off to stake a claim in the wild territory of ourselves. Now we're proving it up.

I ask if he wishes he knew what happened to Huck, afterward.

> *Why?*
> So we'd know what to do.
> *Dad, we're writing our own story!*

And so we are. Like birds that fly through the sound of their own calling, we hadn't realized it. A few days later Lonnie asks what I dream about. I tell him I don't remember dreams very often, and that maybe I don't dream at all. He laughs.

> You're dreaming right now.
> *What?*
> I remember, before we moved, you told somebody we were gonna be living our dream.

He's right again. Twain says that in dreams, "we do make the journeys we seem to make: we do see the things we seem to see; the people, the homes, the cats, the dogs, the birds, the whales, are real . . ." We have given ourselves over to what dreams and story have made possible, their attentive care, their eloquent keeping.

About This Story

Samuel Green is a native of Washington and was the state's first poet laureate in 2007. He and his wife live off the grid in a log house they built on Waldron Island, one of the smallest and most remote islands in the San Juan archipelago. There they run Brooding Heron Press and Bindery, where Samuel is the editor and bookbinder, and Sally is the book designer and printer—together creating beautiful limited edition books of verse by the likes of Gary Snyder, Ted Kooser, and Jane Hirshfield.

We loved how Green's poem "Island Potluck," originally published in his 2020 collection, *Disturbing the Light*, and his essay "Into the Territory," originally featured in the anthology *Night Lights*, show both extremes of island living—the isolation and the sense of community it affords. "Island Potluck" captures an event much like the rituals we learned about in other nearby communities. For example, every fall on Shaw Island, residents gather apples from across the island and sell cider and baked goods. The money they raise sends the island's eighth graders to Washington, DC on a field trip.

Paddling with Spirits

IRENE SKYRIVER

Excerpted from *Paddling with Spirits: A Solo Kayak Journey*

After my first few strokes out into the channel, I stopped to look behind. On the Ketchikan skyline loomed the enormous sky-scraping cruise ships. They seemed such beasts of human creation. They represented everything I wished to escape. As I looked ahead toward the gray mist-enshrouded channel, I had no idea what encounters might lie ahead, but there a salmon jumped and splashed on the surface of the water. I chose the way of the salmon and paddled off. . . .

The next morning dawned clear and serene, and I was on the water early. I paddled along the shore and across a wide body of water. Then, when a slight NW wind rose behind me, I decided to sail. I had an inverted triangular sail with tethers that attached to either side of my paddle. So all I needed to do was hold the paddle and spill-off extra wind or adjust for direction by turning the sail to the degree that I was able. This had limited applications but was a fun break from paddling. It was my first try at sailing on the journey, and I found it relaxing after the exertion of the crossing. At first the going was slow but then the wind picked up enough to move me right across the bay to Foggy Point. It was late morning when I reached the other side and went ashore for a snack. Because I was well rested from sailing, I decided to head back out. Now the gill netters were out in full force, fishing from Foggy Point all the way down to the Alaskan-Canadian border.

I found the glut of fishing vessels very interesting. Earlier in the summer when I was planning my trip, my friend Bob Lyon, who'd done a solo paddle around Vancouver Island, told me about a psychic he'd consulted before his voyage. Her name was Laurie McQuary and she came highly recommended. Since she lived in Idaho, I assumed she was unfamiliar with the Northwest coast, so I'd been a little skeptical about her ability to divine my route with any degree of accuracy. However, if I would travel on faith that my ancestor spirits were with me, why not put merit in a psychic's skills? I sent my itinerary by mail and she returned it marked with comments that I had, in some cases, questioned as I read. Her first warning along my route was here at Foggy Point. She wrote I would have some sort of "interference or slight inconvenience with heavy boat traffic." How, I thought, could I have "heavy boat traffic" in the middle of nowhere? But sure enough, her predictions were accurate. Gill netters with cork lines stretched out, made it impossible to not paddle right over their gear. As she had noted, it really was not much of an inconvenience. But it certainly encouraged me to take her other predictions seriously.

Far from being a problem, really, the fishermen hailed me with well-wishes as I paddled by, and when I stopped to talk to one he offered to let me use his marine radio to put a call through to Gregg back on Lopez. I went aboard and soon an operator had me patched through, loud and clear to Gregg and my son Raven. What a joy it was to talk to them! It had been eight days since I'd left Lopez, but it felt like so much more. Not only did I feel triumphant at having spoken to my family, but the kind fisherman gave me a pair of sunglasses too, which I happily received, since mine had sunk to the sea floor earlier in the day. And to top it all off, he sent me away with a gorgeous slab of fresh caught king salmon.

After many heartfelt thanks I paddled another five miles in choppy water and ducked into a last-chance sort of cove with a wonderful shell beach covered with deer and cougar tracks. The water of the cove was a brilliant blue-green. In this lovely setting I made a feast of my salmon fillet. A logger would have been hard-pressed to eat as much as I did that night. . . .

• ✦ •

That night I had a dream. I was flying, soaring just over the treetops. I was able to do this by simply bounding upwards. I often had flying dreams, but this time the reason I took off above the trees was to escape some very evil force. The "force" appeared as a sort of wild energy, throwing off intense light and moving at super-human speed through the woods below me. Finally I realized that I had to come down and confront the energy because it was about to harm someone innocent.

I tossed in my tent and awoke wondering: were my ancestors trying to communicate a looming danger? Unfortunately the dream had begun to blur right away. I couldn't remember more details, and I fell back to sleep. . . .

• ✦ •

I was up at 4:00 A.M. The sky was still moonlit. I made a fire for tea and pancakes and was gone by 5:30. Gale-force winds were forecast, and once away from Penrose I would be laid open to the full wilds of the sea. For the next few days, the Queen Charlotte

Sound and the Pacific beyond would be all there was to be seen to the west. To be prudent, early morning departures were a must. I paddled hard to Kelp Head where it was wild with huge rolling sea swells, but I was relieved that there were no breakers. After making it around to the south side I decided the conditions looked good enough to go for Cape Caution, about eight miles further. From there, I paddled toward Blunden Bay on the cape.

As I made my careful approach to the bay through large swells and increasing winds, grey whales spouted like geysers all around me and their immense bodies rolled at the surface. I could hardly appreciate the grandeur of the scene because with every stroke I was concentrating with all my power on riding the roller-coaster waves without mishap. Even though I knew whales were all around me I could not concern myself with the possibility that one could surface right under me.

At last, I surfed into a long sandy beach. Fresh wolf tracks were everywhere. Though I was unlikely to hear them above the pounding surf, I hoped I'd have a chance to see them.

I lay on the beach that evening and watched the whales spout. While the hypnotizing, pounding surf pulsed in my tired body, I thought of the shadowy stories of my mother's ancestors, some of whose origins were from down the coast in Washington. They had hunted whales from canoes not much bigger than my kayak. With soft sands under me, rhythmic surf and whale breath blowing in from the bay, I felt enveloped by my mother's ancestor spirits, and pulled to another shore in another time. . . .

• ✦ •

I left my bandit camp and paddled into a brilliant morning amidst ferry traffic between the islands of Mayne, Galiano, Saturna and Pender, and then through Navy Channel. The day was calm, with winds only at the headlands. I came through Plumber Channel, the exit of the Canadian Gulf Islands to look across the glassy-still Haro Strait and Boundary Passage. I would be in the San Juan Islands by the afternoon!

Haro Strait can be harrowing but the spirits that guided me now granted a most benign crossing. Tankers ran these waters like a superhighway, and two passed through when I was about a third of the way across. I saw another in the distance. These ships moved fast, and having seen the first two pass, I could roughly calculate that this third one would come quite close at the rate I was going. I poured on the coals in hope of not being mid-channel when the monstrosity plowed through. It never would have noticed little ol' me out there. In fact it did come a little too close for comfort, but I already had my sights set on Waldron Island, its long sweeping sandy beach ready to embrace me like a loving arm. After nineteen miles of paddling I pulled onto the shore of my friend Laurie Glenn's charming and funky little beach-house property. I was back in the US of A!

Two friends of Laurie's were on the beach and were probably a little shocked at my bold and half-naked landing right at their feet. Soon they and eight visitors of Laurie's were on the beach welcoming me. They had not known I was coming and in fact the friends were gathered for a send-off to Laurie who was about to sail north with her partner for two months. My timing was impeccable. If I'd come a day later not a soul would have been there. As it was, before I was even out of my kayak, I was handed the juiciest, fattest fig I had ever seen. It was just plucked from the tree and very ceremoniously given to me with a deep, reverent bow. Even though they were not expecting me they knew instantaneously that this was a momentous occasion for me. These people were part of my extended tribe. They are people that we Lopezians celebrated special occasions with. Waldron has no ferry service, so these people are fringe of the fringe. My people!

That night, their house glowed like a lantern as the send-off party swung into full motion. Joyous laughter pealed, but my energies were depleted and I bedded down for the last night of my journey under a starlit sky. I had called Gregg to tell him that I estimated arriving at Odlin Park on Lopez at about noon, and that night I hardly slept.

• ✦ •

In the morning, I loaded my boat, tucked my lifejacket (still not worn once) in its place behind me and pushed off quietly from the soft sands of Laurie's beach. There was not a peep from the house. I had about fifteen miles to paddle to get to Lopez and I could see right off that I was really going to have to work hard to prove I belonged there. My eyes watered in the sharp headwind. I crossed President Channel and rounded Orcas Island to its southern shoreline. Here I experienced the heaviest boat traffic of my 750 miles. Power boats between Orcas and Shaw Islands ran like a pack of rats back to their homeports along the coastal mainland. It was August 18th. Summer was drawing to a close and we, one and all, needed to get back home! I dodged their nasty wakes and pushed on through the unrelenting wind, thinking of my many encounters with magic and mystery, with obstacles great and small. I thought of the endless acts of kindness bestowed on me by the very humans of whom I had grown to be cynical. I knew that all of this had come my way because I had opened myself to trust and faith in the power and loving guidance of my ancestors. I was carried by my understanding of their actual lives;

lived in undoubtedly harsher times along this coast. Their lives and struggles were omnipresent, a great source of inspiration when I needed the courage to press on. My father and mother had both suffered much in their lives, and only ever wished for me to be happy. The wisdom of their uncomplicated love and advice was and had always been a great and empowering source of motivation.

• ✦ •

One of the final predictions from the psychic had been that this journey would reveal a "strong metaphysical connection" between my father and me. I could not deny the accurateness of her otherworldly readings; it was one more level of the magic that had aligned to guide me on this spirit quest. There's no way she could have known about the white hummingbird-spirit-of my-father, who initially lent me the reassurance to proceed with my daring dream.

Now, I was coming home reaffirmed in my desire to commit to my tribe, the close and supportive community we lived among. I was thankful for the love and support of my beautiful family and community for having helped to give me the permission, the courage, and the faith to make my desire into a reality. I thought of how our society at large lives in fear. How can we teach our children to love and care for the Earth when they are afraid to be out in the magic of her wilds? My solo journey had reaffirmed above all my yearning to live an ecstatic rather than a fearful life.

As I drew near to Lopez Island I could hear faint sounds of drums reverberating and a saxophone squawking joyful rifts. Yes! There was my tribe; there were my loves! They lined the beach. Children ran this way and that. Friends sang and shouted out. I stopped mid-channel just to cry. I then paddled with all my strength, driving my bow up onto the sandy shore to the tremendous embrace of my community and family. I jumped from my kayak and first kissed the ground and then kissed my man, my daughter and my sons and looked to the blue sky and gave a thanks to the spirits of my ancestors. I was home!

About This Story

Drawn to its alluring cover picturing a wooden boat with an otter alongside under a starry sky, we couldn't help picking up Irene Skyriver's award-winning book *Paddling with Spirits: A Solo Kayak Journey* in the Lopez Bookshop on Lopez Island. Her book is a compelling read from front to back, recounting her physical and emotional journey as she makes her way from Ketchikan, Alaska, to her home on Lopez Island in the San Juans. We follow Skyriver as she encounters harsh weather, wolves, bears, whales, and the wild beauty of the coastal waters while also weaving in a narrative of her relationships and stories passed down from her ancestors.

Born in Port Townsend, Washington, of Tlingit, Makah, and European heritage, Skyriver has lived on Lopez Island since 1980, having moved there with her children and horses to live off-grid as a single parent. Beyond writing, she's a poet, a dancer, and a singer of traditional "Earth Circle Songs." Irene is a heartbeat of the community on Lopez, where she has organized annual parades for Earth Day and International Women's Day, and was an early founder of rites of passage ceremonies for the youth, and Summer and Winter Solstice celebrations.

SAN JUAN ISLANDS NATIONAL WILDLIFE REFUGE
EASTSOUND
WALDRON ISLAND
MORAN STATE PARK
A
B
2
1
TURTLEBACK MOUNTAIN PRESERVE
SPIEDEN ISLAND
C
D
ORCAS ISLAND
YELLOW ISLAND
H
J
ENGLISH CAMP
SHAW ISLAND
10
BLAKELY ISLAND
SAN JUAN ISLAND
SPENCER SPIT STATE PARK
FRIDAY HARBOR
I
E
9
DECATUR ISLAND
LOPEZ ISLAND
5
G
8
6
7
F
AMERICAN CAMP
3
4
SALISH SEA
N
W
E
S
TO SEATTLE

EXPLORE

THE SAN JUAN ISLANDS

✦

A guide for your next San Juan Islands adventure—
on foot, by boat, and by bicycle.

ATTRACTIONS

- **A** Orcas Island Pottery
- **B** Mount Constitution Observation Tower & Visitor Center
- **C** Orcas Island Artworks
- **D** Buck Bay Shellfish Farm
- **E** Barn Owl Bakery
- **F** Cattle Point Lighthouse & Trail
- **G** San Juan Island National Historical Park
- **H** Westcott Bay Shellfish Co.
- **I** The Whale Museum
- **J** Shaw General Store

NATURAL LANDMARKS

1. Cascade Lake & Cascade Falls
2. Mountain Lake & Twin Lakes Trail
3. Watmough Bay
4. Iceberg Point
5. Lopez Hill
6. Shark Reef Sanctuary
7. Mount Finlayson
8. Jakles Lagoon
9. Lime Kiln Point
10. Shaw County Park

What to Do

Hike the trails and beaches.

Being on an island means there is no shortage of coasts with stunning panoramic ocean views, so pack your binoculars and hiking shoes.

Lopez Island is known for its bicycling, but you can explore many of its trails on foot. Head over to **Spencer Spit State Park** for a short walk downhill to a natural sand spit reaching out into Lopez Sound. Its flat trail offers stunning views and bird-watching all day, but consider visiting at dusk as herons catch their last meal of the day in the still and shallow water. **Lopez Hill** is a local favorite with four miles of multiple-use trails for those on foot, bike, or horseback—and offers trails to its summit for those looking for something more challenging. Both **Watmough Bay** and **Point Colville** offer hilly and rocky trails out to stunning beach coves, or you can take an easy, flat forested stroll from the parking lot for the same views. You'll feel transported to another country. Park in the **Agate Beach County Park** lot to take a short, mostly flat hike out to **Iceberg Point** along rocky coastal cliffs with incredible views of the Olympic Peninsula, wildflowers, and passing orcas. For a varied, serene hike along boardwalks in the forest and out to panoramic madrona-lined ocean views of islands with seals, sea lions, and seabirds, take one of our favorite trails to

the **Shark Reef Sanctuary**—an incredible spot to watch the power of the ocean's mesmerizing tides and currents from a safe distance.

Orcas Island offers a more diverse topography and varied terrain, providing an ample range of hikes. After you read "Following Skipjack," take the loop trail at **Obstruction Pass State Park** to the walk-in campsites and go down to the rocky beach. Spend a couple days (or more!) exploring **Moran State Park**, with more than 30 miles of trails. For easier hikes, explore lakeside trails like Mountain Lake Loop and Cascade Lake Loop, and consider taking the adjoining trail to Cascade Falls. For longer and more strenuous hikes, you can hike up **Mount Constitution**, the highest point on the San Juan Islands at 2,409 feet—then climb the steps of the stone tower looking out over the neighboring islands. For the long way up, the Mount Constitution Loop Trail is a nearly 7-mile trek, or for a short but challenging climb, you can take the Little Summit Trail. For something more remote, get away from it all along the Mount Pickett Trail. For glorious vistas, visit Ship Peak Trail at the **Turtleback Mountain Preserve**, or for something more challenging with big rewards, take the preserve's North Trail to reach the turtle's "head"—a rocky headland at the northwest peak of Turtleback Mountain.

San Juan Island offers some of the most scenic coastal hiking. At **Lime Kiln Point State Park**, start out at the interpretive center, then head onto the Loop Trail flanked by madronas, wildflowers, stonecrop, and moss-covered understory along the coast of the Haro Strait to a lighthouse, historic limestone kilns, and a world-renowned viewpoint for whale watching. For fewer crowds, equally stunning sunsets, and views of the resident orcas, you can also visit the adjacent **Westside Preserve**. In the **San Juan Island National Historical Park**, take the forested Jakle's Lagoon nature walk out to Griffin Bay for a peaceful stroll along the beach

with great bird-watching. To extend the stroll, take the turnoff to Mount Finlayson for a nearly 4-mile hike through a variety of different ecosystems. While you're here, stroll the coastal prairie trails of **Cattle Point Lighthouse** to look out for eagles, island marbled butterflies, and foxes. You're also likely to see foxes as you stroll the trails through historic and cultural sites at **American Camp**, where you can take South Beach Trail out to the longest public beach on the island. At **English Camp,** go for an easy hike along the Bell Point Loop Trail or a more moderate hike up Young Hill Trail to an open grassy vista with views of Vancouver Island, Canada.

Shaw Island is mostly privately owned, but you can hike at the **Graham Preserve**, owned by the San Juan Preservation Trust; or at the **Marilyn and Fred Ellis** and **Cedar Rock Preserves**, the University of Washington's biological preserves off Hoffman Cove Road. You can also stroll South Beach along Indian Cove in **Shaw County Park**.

Explore the islands by bike.

Biking the San Juan Islands is a beloved and planet-friendly way to explore the towns, state parks, scenic vistas, and marinas on rolling farm and coastal roads in late spring to early fall when the weather is dry. The ferries are bike friendly, and bike rentals are available in Friday Harbor on San Juan Island, Eastsound on Orcas Island, and in the village on Lopez Island. You can access all of the recommendations in our "Hike the trails and beaches" section by bike—just be sure to pack appropriately with enough food, water, and supplies for more strenuous exercise. Cyclists have all the rights and responsibilities of a vehicle driver on the road, meaning cyclists

need to follow traffic laws. Many of the main roads on the islands have been improved with fog lines (painted white lines separating the road from the shoulder) and widened paved shoulders, but it's still important to wear a helmet and visible clothing.

Lopez Island is a favorite for its smaller, accessible size and less-hilly roads. Consider spending a few days to enjoy the island's hikes, picnics, activities, viewpoints, and cuisine at a leisurely pace. Visit in the spring for the **Tour de Lopez**, an annual tradition since 2004 that has locals and visitors setting out on a variety of routes designed for different biking styles and abilities, and returning to locally crafted food and live music. **Village Cycles** is a family-, Asian-, and woman-owned business in Lopez Village that offers rentals, full service repairs, and sales of bicycles and electric scooters—and will deliver and pick up bikes from the ferry landing.

Orcas Island is a much larger and more challenging island to ride given its steep hills, narrow roads, and fewer shoulders, but worth it for the variety of roads and points of interest. **Moran State Park** has mountain biking trails, and the steep 5-mile ride up Mount Constitution's summit road will really get your heart pumping. Rest your legs and grab a bite to eat on the quieter sides of the island in Olga or Doe Bay. Cyclists on San Juan Island can take a 35-mile loop around the island, with the option to venture out on two scenic routes.

Get out on the water.

Stunning scenery and abundant wildlife can be viewed from out on lakes and the open ocean that surrounds the San Juan Islands. In the islands' inlets, bays, and sheltered coves, you may spot Dall's porpoises, seals, sea lions, river otters, eagles, sea stars, sea urchins, anemones, and—if you're lucky—Southern Resident orcas or humpback whales. There are many ways to get out on the water, whether hopping aboard a tour; chartering a private boat; renting a paddleboard, sea kayak, or canoe; or bringing your own vessel. Local adventure and boat guides, like **Salish Seacrets Adventures** and **San Juan Excursions**, offer private charters and tours with a range of vessel options, including private yacht, sailboat, trawler, dinghy, or inflatable watercraft.

Kayaking is a great way to access small coves, remote beaches, sea caves, and water-access-only islands. Beginners should spend time exploring the calmer waters of protected bays and coves, while more seasoned paddlers can head out to explore islands across the channels or strait. Some consider kayaking around Orcas Island to be safer and smoother than circling the other islands, due to its protected waters in East and West Sound. From Orcas Island's North Shore, paddlers can access several marine state parks—like those on Sucia, Matia, and Patos Islands—where you can relax on secluded shores or hike forested trails.

On Lopez, the water near shore at **Spencer Spit State Park** is generally considered a good place for beginners, and the park offers kayak, paddleboard, and safety gear rentals on summer days and September weekends. From San Juan Island, paddle near **Lime Kiln State Park** for your best chances of seeing resident orcas, or visit a spectacular secluded cove at **San Juan County Park** (you'll need a permit to explore and camp). On Shaw Island, paddle from the less-crowded **Shaw County Park** for chances to see marine life, deer, and birds that favor Shaw's quiet undeveloped shores, or the even tinier 3-acre **Blind Island Marine State Park** just a stone's throw away. You can also follow the **Cascadia Marine Trail**, a

water trail for nonmotorized boaters that connects several campsites across the islands.

Guided kayaking tours with one of the *many* outfitters on Lopez, Orcas, and San Juan Island can get you out on the water safely for a few hours, half or full days, or multiple days. Consider a guided evening paddle from San Juan Island to experience the otherworldly phenomenon of bioluminescence, light reflected or produced by microscopic plankton, jellyfish, and shrimp in dark waters during the warm summer months. For something less strenuous than ocean kayaking, **Moran State Park** on Orcas Island has two freshwater lakes: Cascade Lake and Mountain Lake. Paddle and rowboat rentals are available at the Cascade Lake Day Use Area in summer months, and the lake is stocked every year with rainbow trout, so pack your fishing gear too!

Watch and wait for whales.

Whale watching along island shorelines—where you may see Southern Resident orcas, Bigg's killer whales, humpbacks, gray whales, and minkes—is a truly remarkable and humbling experience. **Lime Kiln State Park**, one the world's best spots for viewing whales from land, offers interpretive information and programs at the visitor center, and a scenic coastal hike to the lighthouse, where you will find a listening station that uses a hydrophone to capture the sounds made by nearby whales. To avoid crowds in summer months, visit the nearby **Westside Preserve** looking out at the same water.

To see whales from the water, you can board large vessels, private charters, or sea kayaks for whale-watching tours, most of which depart from Friday Harbor, San Juan Island. Plan to be out on the water for several hours as you cruise along waiting for whales. Be sure to choose an outfitter that is a member of the Pacific Whale Watch Association, meaning it follows all regulations and guidelines for respectful and safe wildlife viewing.

To enhance your whale-watching experience, stroll through **The Whale Museum** in Friday Harbor, which provides an in-depth look into the natural history of whales, interactive displays on marine conservation, and ongoing research initiatives aimed at understanding and protecting them.

Take in the wonder of wildlife and wildflowers.

The region's rugged coastlines, biodiverse waterways, and protected islands make for a stunning display of wildlife. Besides whales, you may spot Dall's porpoises and river otters in the coastal waters, as well as California sea lions and harbor seals hauled out on the rocks. San Juan Island is home to a population of red foxes—which are also black and brown here—and your best chances for spotting them are around **Cattle Point Lighthouse** and **American Camp**.

While you're there, admire the wildflowers and keep your eyes out for the endangered island marbled butterfly, a species once believed to be extinct, and unique to these islands. Wildflowers on San Juan Island are a sight to behold and worth a visit in the spring. You might spot brilliant purple camas, giant white fawn lilies, or calypso orchids, also known as fairy slippers, casually and quietly blooming to the side of the trail—and broadleaf stonecrop with its bluish-green and red leaves, and yellow flowers draping and sometimes cascading off of rocks. Look for wildflowers blooming in grasslands, prairies, and meadows along trails and coastlines, especially throughout **San Juan Island National Historical Park**, as well as the bluffs on **Mount Finlayson**, **Mount Young**, **Lopez Hill**, and **Turtleback Mountain**.

The islands are also known as among the best places for bird-watching in Washington, and numerous outfitters offer bird-watching tours by land or boat. The many refuges, preserves, and parks—such as the **San Juan Islands National Wildlife Refuge**, the **San Juan Island National Historical Park**, the many marine state parks, **Spencer Spit State Park**, and **Moran State Park**—provide undisturbed and protected habitats for nesting. More than three hundred species of birds have been recorded in the islands, including year-round residents and seasonal visitors migrating along the Pacific Flyway. The Haro Strait and the Strait of Juan de Fuca are summer feeding grounds for seabirds like common murres, pigeon guillemots, rhinoceros auklets, and tufted puffins.

Enjoy the bounty of local farms.

Shop at one of the islands' local Saturday farmers markets, where you can find produce, meat, eggs, bread, and other farm products spring through fall, in addition to locally made crafts, jewelry, pottery, and other goods. **Lopez Island Farmers Market** convenes on the green in Lopez Village, **Orcas Island Farmers Market** at the Eastsound Village Green, and **San Juan Island Farmers Market** at Brickworks community center in Friday Harbor. Be sure to check websites for up-to-date information on times and locations.

Many of the farms also have farm stands and welcome visitors to shop *and* to stay. On Orcas, you can visit **Warm Valley Farm** for organic produce, duck eggs, foraged forest products like mushrooms and berries, and cut flowers, or drop by their weekly market offering other gifts and goods like vintage treasures and skin care products. **Once in a Blue Moon Farm and Lodging**, also on Orcas Island, provides some of the most renowned restaurants in Seattle with fruit and eggs, which can also be picked up at **Island Market** and the weekly farmers market. They offer suites for guests, and a range of farm tours that include petting and playing with goats and sheep in the pasture, gaggling with the geese, hanging with a pig, and feeding an alpaca.

OrcaSong Farm is an organic botanical farm and garden on Orcas Island that makes plant-based, chemical-free aromatherapy products and essential oils. You can visit the lavender fields and the farm store, and even stay at the farmhouse to take in the serene farm setting and breathe in the ocean and lavender winds. On San Juan Island, **Saturn's Return** is a regenerative farm complete with farm stand and farm tours, bed-and-breakfast inn, and venue for weddings, events, and retreats. **Amaro Farm** is a revived historic family-run farm primarily focused on sheep, with a farm store that sells farm and sheep-related items like sheep milk bath products, and agricultural experiences like sheep tours and hands-on farm education. The farm is also home to **Flat Hat Distillery**, crafting whiskey and vodka from the farm's grain and fruit.

Taste the island terroir.

Eat, slurp, and sip at locally-sourced restaurants and sip the San Juans' terroir—the environmental factors like soil, climate, and sunlight that combine and influence flavors. Some of the most delicious and memorable meals we had were those inspired by the flavors distinct to this region.

Buck Bay Shellfish Company on Orcas Island sits on, you guessed it, Buck Bay, where Pacific oysters and clams are raised right across the road from where you can eat them on picnic tables overlooking the bay, in the shade of a massive willow tree. The menu offers other freshly caught seafood as well, like salmon, halibut, and cod—and the deli offers fresh produce, sauces, and seafood to go. **Westcott Bay Shellfish Company** in Roche Harbor on San Juan Island is a working aquaculture farm that raises mussels, manila clams, and oysters—and was easily one of our most memorable stops. Grab lunch at their Tide Tables restaurant, where you'll sit outside to enjoy views of Westcott Bay while you chow down on fresh grilled oysters, smoked salmon toasts, and quite possibly the best chocolate chip cookies you've ever had.

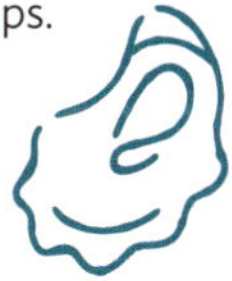

San Juan Islands Sea Salt uses the power of the sun to evaporate pure seawater into a mineral-rich finish for fish, popcorn, cookies . . . you name it! They take their terroir very seriously, producing a madrona-smoked sea salt and a bull-kelp salt, sold locally in stores and at their own store in Friday Harbor on San Juan Island. In Eastsound on Orcas Island, **Girl Meets Dirt** makes heirloom preserves—including jams, shrubs, bitters, and wine—from fruit grown on trees that have been producing fruit for more than a century, boiled down with sugar in copper pots in their kitchen, which you can visit.

The islands are considered a world-class wine region, with bountiful vineyards and orchards. On San Juan Island, **San Juan Vineyard** is a destination winery where you can enjoy a taste of estate-grown wines in a renovated 1895 schoolhouse while listening to live music. For a more intimate affair, **Madrone Cellars and Cider** hosts private tours and tastings on a 40-acre farm, allowing guests to taste their way through the barrels and see the production spaces with the husband-and-wife duo who own the place. **San Juan Island Distillery** produces a range of locally sourced crafted beverages flavored with local botanicals like blackberries, apples, and lavender. For those who prefer beer over vino, **San Juan Island Brewing Company** in Friday Harbor is a gathering place for the community, hosting live music and private events.

On Orcas, **Orcas Island Winery** pours a range of locally grown and crafted wines from a farmhouse tasting room at the base of Turtleback Mountain. **Island Hoppin' Brewery** is Orcas' only microbrewery, and its tasting room in Eastsound offers a rotating list of beer on draft and locally sourced snacks.

The islands' grain farms also support top-notch bakeries. On Lopez, visit **Holly B's Bakery**, a legendary local staple known for its cinnamon rolls, butterhorns, croissants, and hand pies. **Barn Owl Bakery** breads, crackers, bagels, and pastries are available at grocery stores, farm stands, and restaurants across the islands, or at their Saturday farm stand. On Orcas, you can expect lines at **Brown Bear Baking** in Eastsound, which makes small-batch French pastries and leaves guests dreaming of its sourdough boules, croque monsieur, quiche, buns, and seasonal pastries and tarts. On San Juan Island, **Bakery San Juan** provides sourdough breads, breakfast pastries, cakes, and pizzas, with a wine and regional beer shop that'll have you ready for a picnic as you watch and wait for whales.

Take in the island-inspired art.

Artists and artisans are drawn to the island pace of life and inspired by the natural beauty around them. **Island Thyme** makes botanically based skin and body care products—soaps, creams, balms, and herbal oils—on a farm on Orcas Island, with a flagship store in Eastsound. **Orcas Island Artworks Gallery** is a favorite stop on the road to Moran State Park, housed in a historic building once part of a strawberry barreling plant and filled with a large selection of unique art wares from the island's artists and craftspeople.

Drive through the forest to **Orcas Island Pottery**, an island institution since 1945 that built Orcas Island's reputation as a pottery island. Today, it houses wares from dozens of local potters and ceramicists. You'll want to admire the gardens, a giant tree house where kids (and grown kids at heart!) can play, and a view along the waterfront looking out to Waldron Island. **Chimera Gallery** on Lopez is an artist co-op that showcases the island's rich community of artists and their work. If you knit or weave, pick up yarns grown and processed on island from **Island Fibers** on Lopez and **San Juan Island Woolworks** on San Juan.

On a rainy day, consider visiting the **San Juan Islands Museum of Art**, which hosts art exhibitions, education, and programming in a uniquely modern building in Friday Harbor. Also on San Juan Island, **Alchemy Art Center** is a nonprofit offering public events and programs, artist residencies, classes, and youth mentorship programs on its rustic property and around the island in places like the San Juan Island Public Library. **San Juan Islands Sculpture Park** has more than 150 sculptures along five trails that meander through a 20-acre park, and often hosts public events, like their summer art series and monthly guided bird walks from spring through fall.

How to Visit Well

Slow down, breathe deeply, and embrace island time.

While you may try to pack in as much as you can on vacation, the San Juan Islands are all about slowing down to soak in their beauty and get away from the pressures of everyday life. Many island residents and regular visitors suggest a three-day decompression period to shake out the hustle and bustle of the day to day before you're able to let everything go and relax. Before you arrive, do what you can to check out, and limit any external factors that might cause you stress or distraction—like work or personal obligations, communications, and email—so that you can let the island magic wash over you and just be fully present.

This applies to driving, too—it's important to arrive conscious of how fast you're driving and to look out for pedestrians, cyclists, and wildlife who share the rural winding roads. Black-tailed deer, foxes, rabbits, and clever goats and sheep who have found their way past fencing are not an uncommon sight along the roads. The fastest you can legally drive on any island is 45 mph, but in most places the speed limit is 20 to 30 mph. One way to force yourself to slow down is to explore the islands on foot or by bike. You may also want to consider visiting just one or two of the islands and having a deeper experience there instead of trying

to explore them all. And if you're particularly sensitive to crowds and noise, consider visiting during the offseason.

Respect the natural soundscape.

Know that sound and voices travel farther over water, so try to use your indoor voice when outside, and limit the use and volume of music while hanging outside, hiking, or driving. You won't want to miss the incredible natural sounds of the water and animals here—if you're quiet enough, you may even hear a pod of orcas before you spot them. As you're out on trails and beaches, be mindful that locals and many other travelers see these islands as their special place of respite, and maintain a respectful distance and volume. Many parks and campgrounds prohibit the use of generators and motorboats unless electric or solar powered. Drones are not permitted in public parks and conservation areas, and are generally discouraged elsewhere.

Take only memories, leave only footprints.

This catchphrase is attributed to Duwamish Chief Si'ahl (also known as Chief Seattle), who once led the Lushootseed-speaking Southern Coast Salish tribe. The islands receive more than a million visitors a year, a majority of whom ferry over during the sunny and warm summer months, generating a high volume of foot traffic exploring the prairies, meadows, forests, lakes, and shorelines of these resource-strapped islands. When visiting, it's important to look but not touch, and to take only photographs home with you. Stay on the trails and avoid disturbing vegetation, camp only in designated areas, leash and pick up

after your dog, keep your distance from wildlife, and secure items like plastic litter from wind and waves.

To reduce the amount of waste you produce, bring along your own reusable water bottles, coffee mugs, utensils, and bags to shop the farm stands. Limit your purchase of packaged single-serve snacks and beverages, and make time to enjoy your drink or meal on-site to reduce your use of take-out containers. If you're driving, consider hauling trash and recyclables along with you to limit the amount that has to be shipped off island to landfills along the Columbia River on the Oregon and Washington border.

Be safe and mindful when boating.

If you plan to take your own watercraft, practice boat and water safety. Much of the coastal water surrounding the islands is rocky and kelp-forested, and boaters should be aware of challenges like fog, massive container ships barreling down the water highways, and strong underwater whirlpools, tidal currents, and turbulent eddies. Many kayak outfitters stress that in addition to being moderately physically fit, you should stay informed about weather and tidal currents and have the stamina to safely take on these complex waters. Wherever you take your boat, make sure somebody knows your plans, familiarize yourself with navigational rules, and bring a GPS and nautical charts for safe navigation. In the Salish Sea, it's required that you wear a personal flotation device or lifejacket and a whistle or air horn, and highly recommended that you wear or pack a wet or dry suit, a spray skirt, a paddle float, a bilge pump, flares, a first aid kit, and a marine VHF radio. You should always have two forms of communication in a waterproof bag or container.

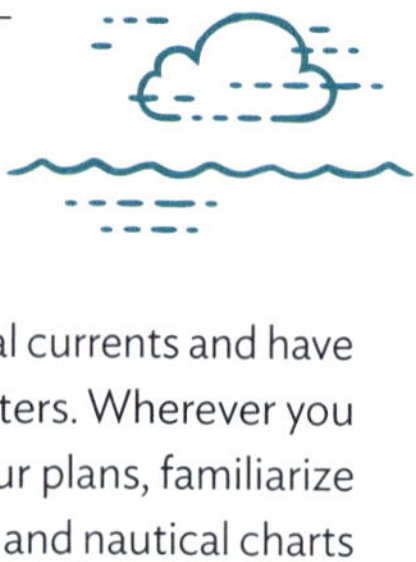

It's also essential to be mindful of the marine residents and keep a safe distance away from them. Be aware of the guidelines and regulations meant to protect marine life. As of 2025, boaters are required to stay 1,000 yards away from Southern Resident killer whales and are asked to keep 100 yards from large whales and 50 yards from other marine mammals like sea lions and seals. The west side of San Juan Island has a year-round voluntary "no boat" zone for recreational and commercial boats along the coastlines around Lime Kiln Point State Park and from Mitchell Point to Cattle Point, to protect the endangered Southern Resident whales' foraging and resting areas. It's best to paddle if you want an up-close look from the water. It's also important to use only designated moorages (like docks and buoys) and avoid anchoring in eelgrass beds, which are vital habitats for fish and shellfish that are eaten by salmon and other wildlife that feed killer whales.

Leave your groceries at home and buy local.

While the inner squirrel in each of us has a tendency to load up the car with everything we might need for a camping trip, believe us, you'll want to leave it at home. The abundant farm stands, grocery stores, markets, co-ops, and bakeries on the San Juan Islands will ensure you'll stay stocked with deliciously fresh and local baked goods, breads, produce, and meats. Depending on the season, you'll also find various markets with freshly caught seafood, like the fish market on the dock in Friday Harbor. Buying local keeps money on the island, supports island families and agrotourism, and helps you meet and build relationships with locals. If you're staying for a week or more, consider placing an order with San Juan Islands Food Hub, an online marketplace with pickup locations across the islands that makes it easy to enjoy food directly from the farms and food producers of Lopez, Orcas, and San Juan.

Conserve water and practice fire safety.

Water, water, everywhere and not a drop to drink. Despite being surrounded by water, the islands have a limited supply of clean freshwater, as they receive far less rain than other areas of the Pacific Northwest due to their position in a rain shadow, and sometimes wells can run dry. While it's important to stay hydrated, be sure to limit your use of water when you can—like when showering and washing clothes or dishes—and consider bringing your own. Note this is especially important in the winter and early spring months, when the public water supply is shut off.

It's also important to obey all fire restrictions and guidelines due to the increased threat of wildfires in the dry summer months. Light fires only in designated campfire rings and pay attention to fire bans. In particular, fireworks are prohibited on land and on boats on the water. Visitors cooking on outdoor grills and smokers should take special care to ensure all fire is out before stepping away.

Familiarize yourself with the ferry system and bring a sense of humor.

Ferries run year-round, several times a day, to the four largest islands: Lopez, Orcas, San Juan, and Shaw. If you plan to drive onto the island, set aside time to plan your comings and goings, and be sure to make advance reservations on the Washington State Ferries website. To avoid the car line,

consider catching a ride or parking your car at the Anacortes Ferry Terminal, walking on board with or without a bike (no need for a reservation, but you'll need to buy a walk-on ticket), and using alternate transportation options on the islands. Transit, shuttles, taxis, and bicycles are available on San Juan and Orcas Islands; Lopez and Shaw do not have public transit or rental car services, but bike delivery or taxi can be arranged when booked in advance on Lopez. Interisland ferries—loaded on a first-come, first-served basis—let you travel between the four islands by car, bike, or on foot. Most of all, be patient. Summer weekend waits to get on the ferry from Anacortes can be two or more hours, and the ferries are infamous for running late due to weather, water conditions, or unpredictable events, so leave yourself ample time.

Consider where you stay.

If you don't plan on camping, support the local community on the islands and avoid adding to the housing crisis by opting for locally owned hotels, motels, inns, resorts, farm stays, and B&Bs instead of short-term vacation rentals not owned by residents of the islands on platforms like Airbnb or VRBO. The islands offer visitors a plethora of unique and historic properties owned by locals and employing island residents, giving an authentic slice of island life. If you use a platform like Airbnb or VRBO, take the time to read the property listing or the host's bio to see if staying there supports their ability to live there (for example, by renting out a room in a home or a guesthouse or barn on a farm) and what they might be doing to support the islands. For example, look for listings that indicate they have a regenerative garden, maintain a native landscape supporting local wildlife, or offer amenities like bikes, boats, or composting for guests.

Islands to Visit

The San Juan Islands are meant to be savored. Locals often share how each island has its own personality, and encourage you to find one or two to explore more deeply—depending on how much time you have—rather than trying to see them all. The four largest islands are serviced by ferry, and other islands of note can be accessed by private boat or with a guide or outfitter.

Lopez Island, affectionately named "Slo-pez" by locals, is a creative, tight-knit community with just about everything you need, and nothing more. Lopez Village, the commercial hub, will charm your socks off. For snacks and groceries, swing by Lopez Village Market or Blossom Grocery. Book lovers flock to the Lopez Bookshop for a curated collection of used and new books. Coffee lovers stop by Lopez Grind with house-made breakfast sandwiches or Isabel's Espresso for pastries from local bakeries. For baked goods, visit Holly B's Bakery or grab a savory baked good to pack for a trail lunch from Barn Owl Bakery. If you're in the village for lunch, rub shoulders with the locals at the El Taco 'Bout It food truck.

According to Lopez residents, the island is best explored by bike. Come by ferry with your own ride or rent one from Village Cycles. For a forested walk out to a beautiful coastal prairie, head out to Iceberg Point or Shark Reef Nature Trail for golden hour. If you're looking for beach time, visit Agate Beach County Park, Odin County Park, or Watmough Bay. End your day at the tranquil Spencer Spit

State Park, with a beach and marshy lagoon habitat great for spotting herons fishing. Once you've worked up an appetite, delight in a bowl of ramen and tasty kimchi from Setsunai Noodle Bar—be sure to make reservations in advance—and end the perfect day with ice cream at the beloved Lopez Island Creamery.

Orcas Island, the largest of the San Juans, is served by a ferry terminal on West Sound, nearly 9 miles from the island's main town, Eastsound. On the way from the terminal to Eastsound, enjoy the unique soundscape and feeling offered by the forested trails of Turtleback Mountain Preserve. Once you get to small but buzzing Eastsound, enjoy brunch at New Leaf Cafe at the Outlook Inn or breakfast to-go from Brown Bear Baking. Enjoy a cocktail from The Barnacle, grab a casual dinner at Mijitas Mexican Kitchen, or go to Matia Kitchen for something innovative and a bit fancier using seasonal local ingredients.

Be sure to shop the amazing selection of books at Darvill's Bookshop and Cafe and the locally made skin care products at Island Thyme. Walk the labyrinth outside Emmanuel Episcopal Church, skip rocks at Eastsound Waterfront Park, and wind your way to Orcas Island Pottery. Venture out in the opposite direction to Moran State Park to see Cascade Falls, hike to the highest point in the San Juan Islands on Mount Constitution, stroll around Mountain Lake, or paddle on Cascade Lake. On your way to Buck Bay Shellfish Company for dinner, be sure to swing through Olga, a tiny hamlet that is home to Orcas Island Artworks.

San Juan Island is the second-largest and most populous of the islands. Its "big city," Friday Harbor, is the commercial center of the whole archipelago. Directly from the ferry dock, you can walk to get a top-notch breakfast at Rocky Bay Cafe and Delicatessen, resupply groceries at Kings Market and grab gear and apparel from their upstairs marine supply store, eat local seafood and farm food at Downriggers, and check out the seasonal catch at the fish market on the Friday Harbor dock. Pick up a book or three at Griffin Bay Bookstore and Cafe, catch a movie at the historic Palace Theatre, and stop by the tiny hole-in-the-wall Crows Nest Coffee for coffee or a breakfast sandwich.

If you have a car, try local farm fresh flavors at the local favorite Duck Soup or Westcott Bay Shellfish Company in Roche Harbor, situated on a working aquaculture farm. While in the area, consider visiting or staying at the historic Hotel de Haro, Washington's oldest continually operating hotel, hosting guests since 1886. Today the resort on the site of a former lime and cement quarry company town offers visitors a glimpse of local history, restaurants, shopping, trails, and a marina.

Shaw Island, the smallest of the ferry-serviced islands, is a good destination for a day trip if you want a taste of small island living. The Shaw General Store has been the hub of the tiny island community since 1924. The store stocks groceries, pantry staples, gourmet goods, books, apparel, locally made products from the islands, and even has a coffee shop that roasts beans on-site with a prototype of the first electric coffee roaster, invented by a Shaw Island resident. In the summer, Captain's Tap Room offers local beer, wine, and live music. Up the road, you'll pass Washington's oldest one-room schoolhouse, which in 2024 had a total of ten students from kindergarten to eighth grade, and the Shaw Island Library and Historical Society, which boasts a small but impressive selection of books. Visit Our Lady of the Rock Monastery or hike the island's several preserves. You can also stroll South Beach, a public beach along Indian Cove at Shaw County Park.

If you have your own boat or decide to go out with a guide or outfitter, good destinations to consider include **Matia and Turn Islands**, which are in the San Juan Islands National Wildlife Refuge and are open to the public for wildlife viewing, hiking, and camping. **Yellow Island** is a tiny 11-acre preserve owned by the Nature Conservancy whose grasslands have been protected from grazing. It's especially worth visiting in spring/early summer when the native wildflowers are in full bloom, including camas, buttercup, paintbrush, chocolate lily, shooting star, and the brittle prickly pear cactus, the only native cactus species in western Washington. From the harbor of **Stuart Island**, you can take the short hike past a historic one-room schoolhouse out to the dramatically situated Turn Point Light Station. If you head to Stuart, you'll want binoculars for a close look at **Spieden Island**, a private island where exotic mammals roam and can be seen grazing along the shore. It was once owned by three Seattle-based brothers—taxidermists and big-game safari guides—who stocked it with Barbary sheep, Corsican goats, Indian jungle fowl, and sika deer for hunting. Ultimately, the endeavor sparked outrage that even caught the attention of Walter Cronkite in a CBS documentary—and the surviving animals were left on the island when the brothers sold it.

Where to Camp

The San Juan Islands offer many marine state parks accessible only by private boat where you can camp, including those on James, Jones, Lummi, Posey, Stuart, Sucia, and Turn Islands. You can also camp on Cypress Island, a natural resources conservation area. In addition to public campgrounds, you can find campsites through online platforms such as Hipcamp that provide access to private land and campsites while supporting local communities and preserving natural spaces.

Lopez Island

Lopez Farm Cottages and Campground, two miles from the ferry terminal, is a farm-style inn with lots of amenities in a 29-acre pastoral landscape with old-growth forests, alder groves, and an organic garden. In addition to cottages, there are reservable walk-in and drive-in campsites. Two sites are dog friendly, but children under fourteen and music are not allowed on the property, to maintain a quiet and tranquil natural ambience.

Odlin County Park is an 80-acre waterfront park on the Cascadia Marine Trail, making it a good stopover for those arriving by paddle, as well as those on foot, bike, or vehicle. Campsites range from forested to oceanfront, just steps away from hiking paths and a kid-friendly bay beach great for paddleboarding and kayaking in calm water. There is a boat launch, a day use dock, boat trailer parking, and five mooring buoys.

Spencer Spit State Park is a 200-acre marine and camping park situated on the Cascadia Marine Trail along a natural sand spit by a saltwater lagoon, with views of Decatur and Blakely Islands. The campground offers tent, RV, and group sites—with several beachside walk-in sites where, if you have a recreational license, you can go crabbing, clamming, and fishing.

Orcas Island

Doe Bay Resort and Retreat is a pristine waterfront property that offers a range of accommodations in a forested setting, including reservable cabins, yurts, domes, and campsites—or some may say, glampsites. If you're looking for luxury experiences on a budget, consider booking one of the campsites and enjoy the on-site spa, cafe, live music, and activities like kayaking and whale watching.

Moran State Park offers the only vehicle-accessible public campgrounds on Orcas Island, with more than one hundred campsites spread across five separate campgrounds along the northern, central, and southern shores of Cascade Lake. Moran's 5,000+ acres offer plenty of recreational opportunities, including lounging on sandy beaches, boating, and hiking up Mount Constitution or out to Cascade Falls.

Obstruction Pass State Park offers ten first-come, first-served primitive walk-in campsites near a stunning pebble beach. The campground is less than a mile from the parking lot on a mostly flat trail, perfect for anyone wanting to try out backpacking.

West Beach Resort, overlooking the Canadian Gulf Islands, offers cabins, RV sites, and campsites in a laid-back resort atmosphere that features beach access, food service, a general store, and a marina with boat rentals. If glamping is more your style, you can stay in an elevated canvas tent cabin with a bed, a futon, a table with chairs, linens, towels, and toiletries. If you plan to pack your own tent, campsites have room for a car, though some require walking in.

San Juan Island

Free Horse Farm is centrally located and offers horsemanship workshops, lessons, training, transport, and equipment, as well as farm stays. Campers can pitch a tent or park a small van on a private knoll among mosses, cedars, and firs. Guests can participate in chores like caring for the horses and tending the garden.

Lakedale is a resort located on 82 wooded acres between Roche Harbor and Friday Harbor, just five miles from the ferry landing. Lakedale's luxury "glampground" has yurts, canvas cabins, and cottages. For a more traditional camping experience, you can reserve classic and family campsites during the summer months. Amenities include a seasonal general store and a bathhouse, and activities including fishing, bocce, swimming, and paddleboarding.

San Juan County Park is comprised of rocky bluffs and gravel beaches looking out on the Haro Strait, making it ideal for sunset views and wildlife spotting. The park is the only public campground on the island and is open year-round for tent and RV camping.

Shaw Island

Shaw County Park is on the southeastern shore of Shaw, with sandy beach access. The campground has thirteen year-round sites, a reservable ball field, and a picnic shelter on a bluff. Dedicated sites are available for Cascadia Marine Trail paddlers, visitors traveling by foot, and campers with hammock tents. RVs and trailers are not advised.

Community Resources

Alchemy Art Center on San Juan Island has worked since 2018 to build a more creative island culture through classes, workshops, events, artist residencies, and free youth programs on-site and out in the community. The Young Environmentalists Program connects youth with artists and activists to explore the intersection of art and environmentalism, while the Youth Mentorship Program pairs them with professional artists to build confidence and develop art skills. ***alchemyartcenter.com***

Be Whale Wise is a collaborative program focused on public education to foster a respectful and sustainable interaction between humans and marine wildlife, particularly whales, in the San Juan Islands. The initiative provides guidelines and regulations for boaters, kayakers, and other marine enthusiasts, which include maintaining safe distances, reducing speed in designated areas, and avoiding "no go" zones to prevent stress and potential harm to the animals. ***bewhalewise.org***

Cascadia Marine Trail (CMT) is a water trail along the Puget Sound that includes an extensive network of more than 60 campsites and 160 day use sites for nonmotorized boaters, with the aim of providing kayakers, canoeists, and small boat sailors with a put-in or takeout spot approximately every three hours. Designated as a National Recreation Trail, it was established by the Washington Water Trails

Association in the late 1990s after members of the local sea kayaking community realized shoreline privatization and development was threatening the five-thousand-year-old tradition of traveling the Puget Sound by small boat.
wwta.org/water-trails/cascadia-marine-trail

Center for Whale Research (CWR) in Friday Harbor is a nonprofit established in 1976 to study and conserve the region's Southern Resident killer whales. By conducting population monitoring, scientific research, and health assessments, the CWR has created the only long-term data set about the Southern Residents' behavior, health, and social dynamics. The CWR also engages in public education and advocacy to raise awareness and promote conservation policies that support ecosystem recovery.
whaleresearch.com

Coast Salish Youth Coalition (CSYC), a program of the Madrona Institute, was founded in 2017 to cultivate the next generation of intertribal Indigenous youth from Coast Salish tribes with ancestral ties to the San Juan Islands. The program provides opportunities to participate in intergenerational cultural events, educational programs, environmental stewardship, and employment that combines Coast Salish traditional ecological knowledge and Western science.
madrona.org/coast-salish-youth-coalition

Friends of Lime Kiln Society (FOLKS) provides recreational, cultural, historical, and educational programs that highlight Lime Kiln Point State Park's diverse marine ecosystem, historic lighthouse, and restored lime kilns. FOLKS promotes the protection of the Southern Resident killer whales commonly viewed from the park,

offering naturalist talks and low tide beach walks, lighthouse tours, student field trips, and an annual Orca Sing and Solstice event in collaboration with The Whale Museum.
folkssji.org

Friends of Moran is a volunteer-run nonprofit that supports Moran State Park and its staff. Using donations and proceeds from the gift shop at the summit of Mount Constitution, Friends of Moran supports a variety of activities within the park, including an annual clean-up event, coordinating volunteer support for park maintenance, and educational opportunities for visitors related to the cultural, historical, and natural environments of the park.
friendsofmoran.org

Lopez Community Land Trust (LCLT), established in 1989 when the cost of housing rose 190 percent in a single year, is focused on building a diverse, sustainable community and fostering a sense of belonging and resilience among residents. LCLT develops and manages affordable housing projects, offers long-term leaseholds that keep land affordable along with resources for sustainable agriculture and community gardens, and promotes other rural development programs that focus on community empowerment and environmental stewardship.
lopezclt.org

Lopez Island Historical Society Museum, in the heart of Lopez Village, is dedicated to collecting, preserving, interpreting, and sharing local history to increase awareness and appreciation of this resource for the benefit of future generations.
lopezmuseum.org

OPAL (Orcas Property and Land) Community Land Trust was established in 1989 to address the critical need for affordable housing and sustainable community development on Orcas Island. OPAL acquires and holds land in trust, develops and manages affordable housing projects, and supports local food production, renewable energy initiatives, and community spaces to create inclusive, resilient communities on the island.
opalclt.org

Pacific Whale Watch Association (PWWA), founded to promote conservation through responsible tourism, consists of ecotourism professionals committed to education and responsible wildlife practices along the coasts of Washington and British Columbia. Member companies adhere to strict guidelines aimed at minimizing disturbance to marine wildlife, particularly whales, which include maintaining safe distances, limiting viewing times, and educating passengers about marine ecology and conservation.
pacificwhalewatchassociation.com

Salish Seeds Project aims to restore native wildflowers and grasses in the San Juan Islands by producing plants and seeds of species native to coastal grasslands, oak savannahs, and rocky meadows, and planting them in San Juan County Conservation Land Bank preserves in partnership with the San Juan Preservation Trust. Master gardeners and other volunteers assist in running the project's nursery, and seeds are occasionally offered to the general public.
sjclandbank.org/the-salish-seeds-project-bringing-back-island-wildflowers

San Juan County Conservation Land Bank was established in 1990 with the mandate to preserve in perpetuity areas in the county that have environmental, agricultural, aesthetic, cultural, scientific,

historic, scenic, or low-intensity recreational value and to protect existing and future sources of potable water. Land Bank staff ensure the careful stewardship of conserved lands for community benefit through conservation easements, preserves, stewardship programs, and joint projects like the Salish Seeds Project.
sjclandbank.org

San Juan Historical Society and Museum shares and interprets the story of the peoples of San Juan Island through its collections, programs, and publications. Both the historical society and the museum work to collect, preserve, and exhibit historical data, information, and artifacts to honor the island's heritage and help residents and visitors learn from the collective experiences of islanders.
sjmuseum.org

San Juan Islands Food Hub is an online marketplace allowing customers on Lopez, Orcas, and San Juan to buy directly from local farmers and food producers through one convenient storefront and receive their orders weekly at a pickup location on each island. The cooperative's mission is to increase the production and sales of local food in San Juan County, support a viable agricultural economy, strengthen food security, and promote access to healthy, sustainably grown food.
sjifh.com

San Juan Preservation Trust (SJPT), founded in 1979, is dedicated to conserving and protecting the natural landscapes and heritage of the San Juan Islands. It works to acquire land and conservation easements in collaboration with landowners, government agencies, and the community in a joint effort to safeguard critical habitats, scenic vistas, and cultural sites, and to maintain intact accessible land for future generations.
sjpt.org

SeaDoc Society is a UC Davis program based on Orcas Island, dedicated to the health of the Salish Sea's marine wildlife and ecosystems. Its scientific research uncovers environmental factors that threaten the web of life, provides information to the public and policy makers, and serves as a catalyst for taking action and finding solutions that improve management, policy, and restoration efforts. ***seadocsociety.org***

Superpod is an international gathering of scientists, filmmakers, authors, journalists, former trainers, naturalists, orca advocates, and people who want to see killer whales in their natural home. The public event combines whale watching, learning, sharing ideas, and taking actions that help protect orcas and bring an end to cetacean captivity. ***superpod-event.com***

The Whale Museum in Friday Harbor is dedicated to promoting stewardship of whales and the marine environment through education and research. The museum serves as a hub for scientific research, educational programs, and public outreach focused on marine mammals, particularly the Southern Resident orcas. It features exhibits showcasing the natural history of whales, interactive displays on marine conservation, and ongoing research initiatives aimed at understanding and protecting these majestic creatures. ***whalemuseum.org***

Wolf Hollow Wildlife Rehabilitation Center is dedicated to the rescue and release of injured and orphaned wildlife across the San Juan Islands. The center offers public education programs about the impacts of human activities on local ecosystems and provides medical care and rehabilitation for injured birds, mammals, and reptiles so they can return to their natural habitats. ***wolfhollowwildlife.org***

Essential Reads

The Salish Sea: Jewel of the Pacific Northwest
by Audrey DeLella Benedict and Joseph K. Gaydos (Sasquatch Books, 2015)

Living High: An Unconventional Autobiography
by June Burn (Duell, Sloan and Pearce, 1941)

Writer in a Life Vest: Essays from the Salish Sea
by Iris Graville (Homebound Publications, 2022)

Diary of the One Swelling Sea
by Jill McCabe Johnson (MoonPath Press, 2013)

Reflections on Life in the San Juan Islands
by Mary Kalbert (Dream Lake Publishing, 2016)

Storm Boy
by Paul Owen Lewis (Tricycle Press, 1995)

Season Unleashed
by Anna Odessa Linzer (Empty Bowl Press, 2024)

Orca: Shared Waters, Shared Home
by Lynda V. Mapes (Braided River, 2021)

For Love of Orcas: An Anthology
edited by Andrew Shattuck McBride and Jill McCabe Johnson (Wandering Aengus Press, 2019)

Walk Deep
by Abigail Morgan Prout (Wayfarer Books, 2022)

Paddling with Spirits: A Solo Kayak Journey
by Irene Skyriver (Green Writers Press, 2017)

Broken by Water: Salish Sea Years
by Gary Thompson (Turning Point, 2021)

Rainshadow World: A Naturalist's Year in the San Juan Islands
by Susan Vernon (Archipelago Press, 2010)

Acknowledgments

Working on this book series as parents to two young kids has required a village. Ilyssa, first and foremost, would like to thank Dave for supporting and encouraging her enthusiasm for this new *Campfire Stories* series and her decision to *not* plow right into a new job. With Ilyssa taking the lead on travel to research these books, Dave took on the primary responsibility for cooking every meal, doing every school or activity drop-off and pickup for two kids at two different schools, conducting the bedtime routine *every night*, and generally keeping our kids alive, full of snacks, and happy—often for a week at a time. Without Dave's unwavering belief in Ilyssa's passion and ideas, in addition to his editing and writing contributions, there would be no *Campfire Stories.*

We'd also like to thank our dear friend Sarah Low, who hosted and accompanied Ilyssa on this trip, made an impressively detailed trip plan and spreadsheet, lured her to every island bakery for "just a taste," reminded her to slow down and lean into the pace of island time (while somehow also walking extremely fast?), and served as a personal ecologist—earnestly and enthusiastically answering every "What's this?!!?" question. And we'd like to thank Ilyssa's mom, Diane Shapiro, who also supports us during these times of travel and writing, and our many friends who host the girls for playdates and sleepovers.

Our daughters, Lula and Isla, deserve thanks for inspiring us to pursue our passions and for their patience and understanding when we have to travel—even when it makes them feel like *a barnacle drifting all alone at sea.*

We are so grateful to Kate Rogers, editor in chief of Mountaineers Books, who curiously continues to entertain our *many* ideas, and—with honesty and great wisdom—helps to refine and shepherd them into the world. We extend this appreciation to the rest of the Mountaineers Books team, whose enthusiasm for our projects is deeply felt—and with a special shout-out to Joleen, who makes us feel like rock stars. To our editing team, Beth Jusino and Lorraine Anderson—we are grateful for your meticulous editorial work, and we admire your ability to take on a massive collection of stories spanning many centuries with enthusiasm and patience.

This series would not be what it is without Melissa McFeeeters, who has been with us from the very beginning and has designed all of our *Campfire Stories* projects—likely the reason you, reader, picked up our book in the first place!

We'd also like to thank the writers, librarians, researchers, and staff and/or volunteers of the many nonprofit organizations and museums we've connected with across the San Juan Islands for your generosity and time. Our understanding of these places would be far less authentic, passionate, and informed without your personal stories, lived experiences and history, and special connections to them. We'd especially like to thank Sarah Pope for the farming education and time with the sheep and your sweet Key; Amy Frost for chatting and opening up the museum to Ilyssa when it was closed; Anne Frances Wysocki for all the island life insights and inviting us to the community meeting; Miles at Shaw General Store for your insights into "Narnia," its unique community, and for the coffee roasting demonstration; Maxine Bronstein for sharing your story and art; Andrew Fleming and Merriss Waters at Saltwater Farm for hosting us and sharing your love for the islands; and Rhea Miller for picking up our cold call, taking us on a hike, and chauffeuring Ilyssa to and from the Lopez ferry when she couldn't resist coming back for one more day.

To the bookstore buyers and staff who take time to chat with us while we're on our research trips, who educate us on local writers and important literature as well as carve a little space on your shelves for our book or feature it in your beautiful, creative displays—we see you and we appreciate you. We can't express how delighted we are to receive texts from friends and family traveling across the US who spot our books or card decks in the wild, or when we ourselves encounter them in real life. It never gets old.

Last, to our dear readers, whose insatiable desire for stories from our wild places allows us to continue collecting stories—we are grateful for your curiosity, love for our natural world, and desire to follow in the age-old tradition of storytelling. Without those readers who reached out or attended our events to say, *When are you going to do MY favorite place in the world?* or challenged us to consider places outside of national parks, we wouldn't have this new series.

Permissions and Sources

Permissions

Benedict, Audrey DeLella and Joseph K. Gaydos. "Jewel of the Pacific Northwest." Copyright © 2015 by Audrey DeLella Benedict and Joseph K. Gaydos. All rights reserved. Excerpted from *The Salish Sea: Jewel of the Pacific Northwest*, by permission of Sasquatch Books.

Burn, June. "Living High." Reprinted with the permission of the estate.

Daley, Michael. "The Child's Song." Originally published in *Moonlight in the Redemptive Forest*, copyright © 2010. Reprinted with the permission of the author.

Gigot, Jessica. "Island Farming." Printed with the permission of the author.

Graville, Iris. "Writing the Interisland Ferry." Adapted and revised from author's previous essays originally published in *Writer in a Life Vest: Essays from the Salish Sea*, copyright © 2022. Printed with permission from the author.

Green, Samuel. "Into the Territory." Originally published in *Night Lights*, printed by Humanities Washington. Printed with the permission of the author.

Green, Samuel. "Island Potluck" from *Disturbing the Light*. Copyright © 2019 by Samuel Green. Reprinted with the permission of The Permissions Company, LLC on behalf of Carnegie Mellon University Press.

Henry, Quincy. "San Juans for the Weekend." Printed with the permission of the author.

Johnson, Jill McCabe. "Following Skipjack." Printed with the permission of the author.

Linzer, Anna Odessa. "Island Light." Printed with the permission of the author.

Priest, Rena. "Remembering Silé at Sxwelisen." Printed with the permission of the author.

Priest, Rena. "Flourishing in the Seasonal Rounds." Printed with the permission of the author.

Prout, Abigail Morgan. "Home of Belonging." Originally published in *Walking Deep*, copyright © 2022. Reprinted with the permission of the author.

Prout, Abigail Morgan. "Marching Orders." Originally published in *Walking Deep*, copyright © 2022. Reprinted with the permission of the author.

Skyriver, Irene. "Paddling with the Spirits." Excerpted and adapted from *Paddling with Spirits: A Solo Kayak Journey*, copyright © 2017. Reprinted with permission of the author and Green Writers Press.

Voigt, Jeremy. "Lime Kiln." Originally published in *For Love of Orcas: An Anthology*, copyright © 2019. Reprinted with the permission of the author.

The editors have made every effort to locate all copyright holders for the excerpts in this book. In some cases, however, they were unable to locate the appropriate person or entity, or to confirm the publication date or other relevant details. If anyone has information on any of the poems, stories, or essays included here, please contact the editors at hello@campfirestoriesbook.com

Sources

Ahearn, Ashley. "EarthFix Conversation: Lummi Tribal Carver Takes Giant Totem Pole on 'Healing' Journey." Jefferson Public Radio

Earthfix, September 26, 2013. https://www.ijpr.org/northwest-environmental-news/2013-09-26/earthfix-conversation-lummi-tribal-carver-takes-giant-totem-pole-on-healing-journey.

Barsh, Russel. "Coast Salish Reef-Net Fishery, Part 1." *Historylink.org*, May 23, 2021. https://www.historylink.org/file/21237.

Boucher, Sienna. "San Juan Islands Inspire Book of Poetry by Gary Thompson." *The Journal of the San Juan Islands*, October 17, 2021. https://www.sanjuanjournal.com/life/san-juan-islands-inspire-book-of-poetry-by-gary-thompson/.

Burkitt, Janet. "Deer Species Finds a Refuge." *The Seattle Times*, July 30, 1998. https://archive.seattletimes.com/archive/?date=19980730&slug=2763866.

Huang, Alice. "Cedar." Indigenous Foundations, accessed April 2, 2025, https://indigenousfoundations.arts.ubc.ca/cedar/.

Lamb, Ron. "Exotic Animals Roam Spieden Island." *Anacortes American*, August 25, 1976. https://washingtondigitalnewspapers.org/?a=d&d=ANACAMER19760825.2.6
3&e=-------en-20--1--txt-txIN-------.

Sx'Wálech to Lopez, Lopez Island Historical Society & Museum, Lopez Island, WA, 2024.

Mapes, Lynda. "The Roar Below: How Our Noise Is Hurting Orcas' Search for Salmon." *The Seattle Times*, May 19, 2019. https://projects.seattletimes.com/2019/hostile-waters-orcas-noise/.

Nalewicki, Jennifer. "Orcas Aren't All the Same Species, Study of North Pacific Killer Whales Reveals." *Live Science*, April 1, 2024. https://www.livescience.com/animals/marine-mammals/orcas-arent-all-the-same-species-study-of-north-pacific-killer-whales-reveals.

The National Park Service. "Kayak." San Juan Island National Historical Park. Last modified July 21, 2022. https://www.nps.gov/sajh/planyourvisit/kayak.htm.

The National Park Service. "Island Marble Butterfly." San Juan Island National Historical Park. Last modified November 13, 2022. https://www.nps.gov/sajh/learn/nature/island-marble-butterfly.htm.

San Juan County Land Bank. "Record $5.2 Million Gift Expands Turtleback Preserve and Returns Some Land to the Lummi Nation." *The Journal of the San Juan Islands,* August 6, 2020. https://www.sanjuanjournal.com/life/record-5-2-million-gift-expands-turtleback-preserve-and-returns-some-land-to-the-lummi-nation/.

Seidman, Lila. "Researchers Propose Two New Killer Whale Species." *Los Angeles Times,* March 29, 2024. https://www.latimes.com/environment/story/2024-03-29/researchers-propose-two-new-killer-whale-species.

Wooten, Tom. "Preserving Our Culture and Our Land through Climate Action." *Native News Online,* November 3, 2023. https://nativenewsonline.net/environment/preserving-our-culture-and-our-land-through-climate-action.

Walker, Richard Arlin. "Traditional Canoes Return to the Waters of the Pacific Northwest." *Source New Mexico,* May 19, 2023. https://sourcenm.com/2023/05/19/traditional-canoes-return-to-the-waters-of-the-pacific-northwest/.

———. "Samish Nation Protects 'Breathtaking' Kelp Forests, Nearshore Habitat." *Salish Current,* November 14, 2023. https://salish-current.org/2023/11/14/samish-nation-protects-breathtaking-kelp-forests-nearshore-habitat/.

———. "Additional Acreage next to Madrona Point to Be Returned to Lummi Nation." *Salish Current,* April 2, 2024. https://salish-current.org/2024/04/02/additional-acreage-next-to-madrona-point-to-be-returned-to-lummi-nation/.

Directory

LOPEZ ISLAND

lopezisland.com

Agate Beach County Park and Iceberg Point
lopezisland.com/directory-2/agate-beach-county-day-park
Mackaye Harbor Rd

Barn Owl Bakery
barnowlbakery.com
108 Grayling Ln

Blossom Grocery
blossomgrocery.com
295 Village Rd

Chimera Gallery
chimeragallery.com
211 Lopez Rd

El Taco 'Bout It
eltacoboutit.com
308 Lopez Rd, food truck next to Isabel's Espresso

Holly B's Bakery
hollybsbakery.com
211 Lopez Rd

Isabel's Espresso
isabelsespresso.com
308 Lopez Rd

Island Fibers
islandfibers.com
4208 Port Stanley Rd

Lopez Bookshop
lopezbookshop.com
211 Lopez Rd

Lopez Creamery
lopezislandcreamery.com
9 Old Post Rd

Lopez Farm Cottages and Campground
lopezfarmcottages.com
607 Fisherman Bay Rd

Lopez Grind
facebook.com/LopezGrind
211 Lopez Rd

Lopez Hill
lopezhill.org
Lopez Sound Rd

Lopez Village
lopezisland.com
265 Lopez Rd

Lopez Village Market
lopezvillagemarket.com
162 Weeks Rd

Odlin County Park
sanjuanco.com/facilities/facility/details/Odlin-County-Park-5
148 Odlin Park Rd

Otis Perkins County Day Park
lopezisland.com/directory-2/otis-perkins-day-park
1396 Bayshore Rd

Point Colville Trail
wta.org/go-hiking/hikes/point-colville
1356 Watmough Head Rd

Setsunai Noodle Bar
setsunainoodlebar.com
45 Eads Ln

Shark Reef Nature Trail
wta.org/go-hiking/hikes/shark-reef-sanctuary
1752–1998 Shark Reef Rd

Spencer Spit State Park
parks.wa.gov/find-parks/state-parks/spencer-spit-state-park
521 Bakerview Rd

Village Cycles
villagecycles.net
214 Lopez Rd

Watmough Bay
lopeztrails.org/watmough-chadwick-colville
Watmough Head Rd

ORCAS ISLAND

visitsanjuans.com/orcas-island

EASTSOUND

The Barnacle
thebarnacle.com
249 Prune Alley

Brown Bear Baking
brownbearbaking.com
29 N Beach Rd #1966

Darvill's Bookshop and Cafe
darvillsbookstore.indielite.org
296 Main St

Eastsound Waterfront Park
sjclandbank.org
96 Main St

Girl Meets Dirt
girlmeetsdirt.com
208 Enchanted Forest Rd

Island Hoppin' Brewery
islandhoppinbrewery.com
33 Hope Ln

Island Thyme
islandthyme.com
310 Main St

Matia Kitchen
matiakitchen.com
382 Prune Alley

Mijitas Mexican Kitchen
mijitasorcas.com
310 A St

New Leaf Cafe
outlookinn.com
171 Main St

Orcas Island Pottery
orcasislandpottery.com
338 Old Pottery Rd

Orcas Island Winery
orcasislandwinery.com
2371 Crow Valley Rd

Salish Seacrets Adventures
salishseacrets.com
340 Brandt-Landing Rd

Turtleback Mountain Preserve
sjpt.org/visit-our-preserves/turtlehead-preserve
1071 Crow Valley Rd

West Beach Resort
westbeachresort.com
190 Waterfront Way

OLGA

Doe Bay Resort and Retreat
doebay.com
107 Doe Bay Rd

Moran State Park
parks.state.wa.us/547/Moran
3572 Olga Rd

Obstruction Pass State Park
parks.state.wa.us/553/Obstruction-Pass
860 Trailhead Rd

Orcas Island Artworks
orcasartworks.com
11 Point Lawrence Rd

SAN JUAN ISLAND

visitsanjuans.com/san-juan-island

FRIDAY HARBOR

Alchemy Art Center
alchemyartcenter.com
1255 Wold Rd

Amaro Farm and Flat Hat Distillery
amarofarm.com
55 Amaro Farm Rd

American Camp Visitor Center
nps.gov/sajh/planyourvisit/american-camp.htm
San Juan Island National Historical Park
4668 Cattle Point Rd

Bakery San Juan
bakerysanjuan.com
775 Mullis St

Cattle Point Lighthouse
nps.gov/places/cattle-point-lighthouse.htm
San Juan Island National Historical Park
Cattle Point Rd

Downriggers
10 Front St

English Camp Visitor Center
nps.gov/sajh/planyourvisit/english-camp.htm
San Juan Island National Historical Park
3905 West Valley Rd

Free Horse Farm
www.freehorsefarm.com
215 Crow Valley Rd

Friday Harbor Seafood
Market on the main dock, summer only
204 Front St

Griffin Bay Bookstore and Cafe
griffinbaybook.com
155 Spring St

Jakle's Lagoon Trail
nps.gov/thingstodo/hike-the-jakyl-s-lagoon-nature-trail.htm
San Juan Island National Historical Park
Trailhead on Cattle Point Rd

Kings Market and Marine
kings-market.com
160 Spring St

Lakedale
lakedale.com
4313 Roche Harbor Rd

Lime Kiln Point State Park
parks.wa.gov/find-parks/state-parks/lime-kiln-point-state-park
1567 Westside Rd

Madrone Cellars and Cider
madronecellars.com
40 First St

Mount Finlayson Loop Trail
nps.gov/thingstodo/hike-the-mount-finlayson-loop-trail.htm
San Juan Island National Historical Park
Trailhead on Cattle Point Rd

Palace Theatre
palacetheatrefridayharbor.com
209 Spring St

Rocky Bay Cafe and Delicatessen
225 Spring St

Roche Harbor Resort and Hotel De Haro
rocheharbor.com
248 Reuben Memorial Dr

Saltwater Farm
saltwaterfarmsji.com
176 Sea Breeze Ln

San Juan County Park
sanjuancountywa.gov/921/San-Juan-Island
15 San Juan Park Rd

San Juan Excursions
watchwhales.com
40 Spring St

San Juan Island Brewing Company
sanjuanbrew.com
410 A St

San Juan Island Distillery
sanjuanislanddistillery.com
12 Anderson Ln

San Juan Island Farmers Market
sjifarmersmarket.com
Brickworks
150 Nichols St

San Juan Island Woolworks
sanjuanwoolworks.com
Oak Knoll Farm
1585 Douglas Rd

San Juan Islands Museum of Art
sjima.org
540 Spring St

San Juan Islands Sculpture Park
sjisculpturepark.com
9083 Roche Harbor Rd

San Juan Islands Sea Salt
sanjuanislandseasalt.com
80 Nichols St

San Juan Vineyard
sanjuanvineyard.com
3136 Roche Harbor Rd

Saturn's Return
saturnsreturn.com
2687 W Valley Rd

South Beach Loop Trail
nps.gov/sajh/south-beach.htm
San Juan Island National Historical Park
Trailhead on Pickett's Ln

The Whale Museum
whalemuseum.org
62 First St N

Westcott Bay Shellfish
westcottbayshellfish.com
904 Westcott Dr

Westside Preserve
sjclandbank.org
296 Westside Rd

SHAW ISLAND

sanjuancountywa.gov/523/Shaw-Island

Blind Island Marine State Park
parks.wa.gov/find-parks/state-parks/blind-island-marine-state-park
Water access only

Captain's Tap Room
shawgeneralstore.com
37 Blind Bay Rd

Cedar Rock Preserve
fhl.uw.edu/facilities-resources/biological-preserves
Park at the preserve gate, where Hoffman Cove Rd dead ends at Hoffman Cove

Graham Preserve
sjpt.org/visit-our-preserves/graham-preserve
Trailhead at Shaw Community Center parking lot, Blind Bay and Squaw Bay Rd

Marilyn and Fred Ellis Preserve
sjpt.org/visit-our-preserves/marilyn-and-fred-ellis-preserve
842 Hoffman Cove Rd

Our Lady of the Rock Monastery
olrmonastery.org
865 Hoffman Cove Rd

Shaw County Park and South Beach
sanjuancountywa.gov/523/Shaw-Island
218 Shaw Park Rd

Shaw General Store
shawgeneralstore.com
37 Blind Bay Rd

Shaw Island Library and Historical Society
shawislandlibrary.org
Blind Bay Rd at Hoffman Cove Rd

SAN JUAN COUNTY

sanjuancountywa.gov

Cascadia Marine Trail
wwta.org/water-trails/cascadia-marine-trail

Cypress Island Natural Resources Conservation Area
dnr.wa.gov/CypressIsland
Water access only

Jones Island Marine State Park
parks.wa.gov/find-parks/state-parks/jones-island-marine-state-park
Water access only

Lummi Island
lummi-island.com
Ferry from Gooseberry Point Ferry Dock, accessible from I-5 north of Bellingham

San Juan County Food Hub
sjifh.com

Spieden Island
Private island (observe only from water en route to Stuart Island)

Stuart Island Marine State Park
parks.wa.gov/find-parks/state-parks/stuart-island-marine-state-park
Water access only

Sucia Island Marine State Park
parks.wa.gov/find-parks/state-parks/sucia-island-marine-state-park
Water access only

Turn Island Marine State Park
parks.wa.gov/find-parks/state-parks/turn-island-marine-state-park
Water access only

Yellow Island Preserve
washingtonnature.org/yellowisland
Water access only

About the Contributors

Audrey DeLella Benedict is a naturalist, guide, science writer, and advocate for research and conservation efforts focused on the effects of climate change on the Arctic and the global ocean. She wrote naturalist guides to the southern Rockies and Great Sand Dunes National Park and Preserve, and the Salish Sea. Her non-profit Cloud Ridge Naturalists, and its publishing arm, Cloud Ridge Publishing, operates with the belief that natural history education inspires and promotes environmental advocacy and stewardship.

June Burn (1893–1969) was an American adventurer, homesteader, and writer known for her love of the Pacific Northwest, particularly the San Juan Islands. Columnist for various Pacific Northwest newspapers, including the *Bellingham Herald,* she eventually started her own the *Puget Sounder*, and wrote an autobiography, *Living High: An Unconventional Autobiography*, chronicling her simple yet rich life, travels, and back-to-nature lifestyle homesteading on Waldron Island.

Michael Daley was born in Boston and earned an MFA from the University of Washington. His poems have appeared in a number of publications and in his poetry chapbooks and collections, including *The Straits, To Curve, Moonlight in the Redemptive Forest, Of a Feather,* and *Born With*. He is also the author of *Way Out There: Lyrical Essays*.

Joseph K. Gaydos is a wildlife veterinarian, surgeon, research scientist, author, and science director of the SeaDoc Society, a marine conservation program at UC Davis. An expert on wildlife health issues, he has traveled the world working on wildlife and ecosystem health, and advises policymakers on issues related to diseases that impact both human and wild animal health, from Washington state to Washington DC.

Jessica Gigot is a poet, farmer, and writing coach who lives on a small sheep farm in the Skagit Valley of Washington. Besides her Nautilus Award–winning memoir, *A Little Bit of Land*, she has published two collections of poetry, including *Feeding Hour*. Her writing and reviews have appeared in the *New York Times*, the *Seattle Times*, and *Orion* magazine. She has a podcast and newsletter titled *Her Deepest Ecologies*.

Iris Graville is the author of four books of creative nonfiction and the publisher of *Shark Reef*, a literary magazine. Her books include *Bounty: Lopez Island Farmers, Food, and Community*, and *Hiking Naked: A Quaker Woman's Search for Balance*, a memoir covering her time in a remote mountain village in Washington's North Cascades after working for twenty years in public health.

Samuel Green served as Washington's first poet laureate (2007–2009) and has published a dozen volumes of poetry, including *The Grace of Necessity*, which won the 2008 Washington State Book Award for Poetry, and *Disturbing the Light*. He has been a college professor and runs Brooding Heron Press with his wife, Sally, out of their off-grid home on Waldron Island.

Quincy Henry grew up near Tacoma, Washington, and was nominated for a Grammy in 2009 for his song "Froglegz N Fishgrease."

He recorded a number of hip-hop albums—including *Declaration of Dopeness*, *The Darkness*, and *Black Gold*—before earning a masters degree in marketing. He and his wife, Whitni, cofounded Campfire Coffee Co. in Tacoma and created the Campfire Explorers Club to help make the outdoors more accessible to everyone.

Jill McCabe Johnson has written three poetry collections—*Tangled in Vow & Beseech*, *Revolutions We'd Hoped We'd Outgrown*, and *Diary of the One Swelling Sea*—as well as narrative nonfiction and fiction. She teaches creative writing at Skagit Valley College and co-owns Kangaroo House Bed and Breakfast Inn in Eastsound. She is also founder and editor-in-chief of Wandering Aengus Press.

Anna Odessa Linzer is a writer of nonfiction and author of the poetry collection *Season Unleashed* and four novels: *Ghost Dancing*, which received an American Book Award, *Blind Virgil*, *Dancing on the Water*, and *A River Story*, which were collected in the trilogy *Home Waters*. Linzer, who has always lived along the Salish Sea, has also worked as a bookbinder, book designer, and editor.

Lynda V. Mapes has been a reporter at the *Seattle Times* since 1997, focusing on coverage of Native tribes, nature, and the environment. Her books include *Orca: Shared Waters, Shared Home*, winner of a 2021 National Outdoor Book Award and a 2022 Washington State Book Award; *Witness Tree: Seasons of Change with a Century-Old Oak*; and *Elwah: A River Reborn*.

Rena Priest earned an MFA from Sarah Lawrence College and served as Washington State's sixth poet laureate (2021–2023) and as a judge for the 2024 National Book Awards. She is the author of *Northwest Know-How: Beaches* and the poetry collections *Sublime Subliminal* and *Patriarchy Blues*, winner of an American Book Award. She also edited the anthologies *I Sing the Salmon Home* and *The Larger Voice*.

Abigail Morgan Prout grew up as a wild island child on Lopez Island in the Salish Sea, and surprised herself by returning to raise a family here. *Walk Deep*, her first book, won the 2021 Homebound Publications Poetry Prize, a 2023 Nautilus Book Award, and was nominated for a Pushcart Prize. It is a love letter to Lopez Island, specifically to a forest path on Lopez Hill that functions as her muse. Abigail is passionate about the role that nature and writing play in personal transformation and leadership. Abigail lives with her husband, Clive, and their children, Iona and Jax, in the forests and on the beaches where she played as a child.

Irene Skyriver is the author of *A Woman's Life on the Edge of the Sea: Four Decades of Poetry* and the novel *Paddling with Spirits: A Solo Kayak Journey*. She moved with her children and horses to Lopez Island in 1980 and has lived off the grid since then.

Gary Thompson has written six books of poetry, including *Broken by Water*, *One Thing After Another*, and *To the Archaeologist Who Finds Us*. With an MFA from the University of Montana, he taught creative writing at California State University, Chico, for more than twenty-five years.

Jeremy Voigt is the author of the book *Something to Carry Home and Not Kill* and two chapbooks: *Neither Rising nor Falling* and *The Invisible Heart of Everything*. He has been nominated for a Pushcart Prize, was featured on *The Writer's Almanac*, and was runner up for the 2019 Discovery Poetry Prize. He is a high school English teacher and adjunct professor. He lives by a large lake in western Washington with his wife and three children.

About the Editors

Ilyssa Kyu is the founder of Amble, a sabbatical program for creative professionals to take time away with purpose in support of nature conservancies. She is a design researcher and strategist with a degree in industrial design and previously worked at boutique and global design studios. She is currently using her design consulting experience to support nature nonprofits through All Hands, a creative collective, as well as continually dreaming up ways to integrate her love for storytelling and the outdoors.

Dave Kyu is a socially engaged artist and writer. Born in Seoul, South Korea and raised in the United States, he explores the creative tensions of identity, community, and public space in his work. He has managed public arts projects for the Asian Arts Initiative, Mural Arts, and the City of Philadelphia. His own creative projects have found him commissioning skywriting planes to write messages 10,000 feet above Philadelphia and doing everything Facebook told him to do for a month.

Together, they've created *Campfire Stories: Volume I*, *Campfire Stories: Volume II*, *Campfire Stories Card Deck*, and *Campfire Stories Card Deck—For Kids!* They were artists-in-residence at Independence National Historical Park as part of the Imagine Your Parks grant—a collaboration between the NEA, the National Park Service, and the Mural Arts Program that resulted in an event, "I Will Hold You in the Light," which brought together six diverse performers responding to the theme of "The Pursuit of Happiness."

MORE CAMPFIRE STORIES

Campfire Stories bring together the beauty of the natural world and the traditions of storytelling across cultures in order to build deeper connections to our public lands.

Tales & Travel Companions:

The Adirondacks
Cape Cod
Chesapeake Bay
The Redwood Coast
The San Juan Islands
Santa Fe & Taos

• ✦ •

Tales from National Parks and Trails:

Campfire Stories
Campfire Stories, Volume II

• ✦ •

Cards to Ignite Imagination:

Campfire Stories Deck
Campfire Stories Deck for Kids!